GERMAN PANZER
MARKINGS
From Wartime Photographs

GERMAN PANZER
MARKINGS
From Wartime Photographs

Ian Baxter

The Crowood Press

First published in 2007 by
The Crowood Press Ltd
Ramsbury, Marlborough
Wiltshire SN8 2HR

www.crowood.com

British Library Cataloguing-in-Publication Data
A catalogue record for this book is available from the British Library.

ISBN 978 1 86126 897 6

Photograph captions:
Page 2: See page 90
Page 5: Russia, summer 1941: passing a burning building, a crewman wears a
steel helmet as he rides outside the turret of his PzKw III Ausf J. Below and
behind the single tactical number '7' marked on the dark grey (RAL 7021) paint
of the turret in broken, stencilled style, the white outline bison badge of Panzer
Regiment 7, 10. Panzer Division can just be made out on the original print.
Note also the pennant on the radio antenna, apparently triangular and in stripes
of black, white and red.
Page 7: Russia, summer 1943: an SdKfz 251 Ausf D half-track races past blazing
Soviet equipment. The licence plate 'WH-640929' is painted directly on to the
dark yellow (RAL 7028) finish of the front plate, in black on an unbordered
white strip.

Edited by Martin Windrow
Typeset by Jean Cussons Typesetting, Diss, Norfolk
Printed and bound in Great Britain by Biddles Ltd, King's Lynn

CONTENTS

FOREWORD

THE German Wehrmacht of World War II will always be associated with armoured warfare; in their campaigns on the Western and Eastern fronts and in North Africa, Germany's armies were spearheaded by the tanks and other armoured fighting vehicles of the Panzer (armoured) and Panzergrenadier (mechanized infantry) divisions. This book offers the reader a collection of photographic evidence for the use of a wide range of types and examples of markings on the tanks, other AFVs and some supporting vehicles used by these formations and units. As well as conventional Army (Heer) tank units, it includes a number of subjects of particular interest, such as Panzer and Panzergrenadier units of the Waffen-SS, Tiger tank battalions, and self-propelled assault gun (Sturmgeschütz) units.

All the types of markings displayed on these vehicles to distinguish them on the battlefield evolved over the war years, and this book illustrates a number of those changes, both of design and application. During the German rearmament programme of the 1930s few markings were used; but as German military organizations increased in size and complexity during the preparations for war, systems of markings to denote unit and sub-unit identity and organization were developed. In total there were up to nine types of distinguishing markings or signs that could be applied to the military vehicle (in addition to small technical stencils), although most never carried all of these. The main types were: national insignia; tactical numbers, identifying the vehicle and sub-unit at a distance; formation and/or unit insignia; on armoured vehicles other than tanks, tactical symbols identifying sub-unit types, based on conventional map symbols; licence plates, and command pennants. To these might be added temporary air recognition markings and flags; and, at the initiative of individual crews, vehicle names, and tallies of victory markings.

The variations in the use of these markings seen during the war were both regulated and unregulated. The simplest reason for such variations was sheer practicality: when combat attrition was running at high levels the need to get replacement vehicles into action quickly took priority over applying regulation insignia. Some designs or methods of application were ordered to be changed by central authorities; some of these orders were obeyed, others disregarded – old or unofficial markings were sometimes tolerated at unit or even individual level, especially in the case of those with respected combat records. A number of divisions were ordered to change or even remove their insignia to disguise troop movements, especially prior to a major offensive, and in some units such changes became permanent. Others repainted their insignia following a battle or a long march. Divisional insignia might be seen painted in different colours, both official and unofficial; and even national insignia were sometimes painted in unofficial styles.

The tables of organization of all German formations changed many times during the war, and markings changed as well in order to keep pace. Panzer division insignia were altered on average about once a year; older designs were changed and updated, and new symbols and insignia were introduced to accommodate the changing orders of battle. By 1943 some units were being sent to the front with incomplete markings, and there were those that carried virtually none – even when ordered to do so. Consequently, photographs of these vehicles lead to a certain amount of confusion. With vehicles of some units not all carrying the same markings, and others not showing any markings at all, it is sometimes impossible to identify from photographs the areas where these vehicles were operating. Nevertheless, it is believed that the photographs in this book provide a useful overview of the marking practices of the major German armoured formations, and that they include a reasonable range of variations in the details of such practices on various fronts at various dates.

The basic camouflage colours adopted before and during the war years were few in number, but the variations seen in the field were considerable – and after the change to a three-colour system in 1943, when units and even individual crews were responsible for their application, they became literally innumerable. The monochrome photographs in this book show a comprehensive range of examples; and these are supported by the illustrations in the colour section, together with a few very rare wartime colour photographs.

Acknowledgements

It is with the greatest pleasure that I take this opportunity to thank those who helped make this volume possible. My first expression of gratitude goes to my friend and fellow photograph collector Rolf Halfen. He has been an unfailing source, supplying me with the bulk of the Panzer collection from numerous private albums that have been shut away for many years. Rolf has searched out and contacted numerous collectors across Germany, and it is only his patient persistence that has unearthed examples of some of the rarer vehicles.

Further afield, I am also extremely grateful to Marcin Zboiska in Poland, my Eastern Front photographic specialist, who supplied me with a number of rare images obtained from a private collector in the Ukraine; these show a number of interesting models including late variant Panzerkampfwagen IVs, Panthers and Tigers. I am also indebted to my dear friend Richard Markey from Scotland, who worked painstakingly to digitally enhance the colour photographs and brought back to life these very rare colour images.

Finally, I wish to express my appreciation to my illustrator and good friend Rachael Hudson for her careful and accurate work.

Credits

Unless otherwise credited, all photographs in this book are credited to the HITM Archive – *www.hitm.archive@tiscali.co.uk*

I would like to thank Christian Ankerstjerne of *Panzerworld* for his help on the *Zimmerit* pattern illustrations, which have been adapted and reproduced from his original illustrations.

Illustrations are by Rachael Hudson of R. Hudson Illustrations – *Rachaelhudson@hotmail.com*

Photographic colour and digital enhancement by Richard Markey – *rm-design@hotmail.co.uk*

INTRODUCTION
German Armoured Formations

O N 16 March 1935, Germany, under the National Socialist government led by Adolf Hitler, formally announced that it would no longer observe the disarmament provisions of the Versailles Treaty of 1919, which had – among many other limitations – forbidden the acquisition of tracked armoured fighting vehicles. This announcement was followed by universal military conscription; and by a massive rearmament programme, in which the building up of a strong force of armoured units figured prominently. This had been anticipated for years, and secret research and training had long been carried out with the aid – ironically enough – of Soviet Russia.

The best use of tanks in any future war had been a subject of lively discussion in the armies of the major powers for many years. One school of thought drew upon experience in World War I to argue that while some fast, light 'cavalry' tanks could fill the traditional scouting and screening role of mounted troops, the bulk of the armour should be slow, heavily armoured 'infantry tanks', widely dispersed to support the advance of the infantry by destroying the enemy weapons emplacements which stood in their way. However, in Germany these conservatives eventually lost the argument to the enthusiasts for a much bolder vision. This saw the tanks concentrated into fast, mobile, more or less self-sufficient formations of mixed arms – tanks, supported by motor-towed artillery and infantry carried in motor vehicles – which could operate independently of the mass of the marching infantry and the slow 'rear echelons', to punch holes in the enemy front and exploit forwards to wreak havoc in his rear areas.

The task of building a strong force of medium and heavy tanks took German industry several years, but in the meantime light types were produced and used for tactical training. The first three German armoured divisions – 1., 2. and 3.Panzer Divisionen – were formed in October 1935, the 4. and 5. in

November 1938. All these, and some separate armoured units, fought in the brief Polish campaign of September 1939, and following this victory more divisions were converted to the armoured role: the 6., 7., 8., 9. and 10. had joined the Panzerwaffe by the time the Wehrmacht was unleashed on the Low Countries and France in May 1940.

*   *   *

Victory in the West led to a doubling of the Panzer formations, with 11., 12., 13., 14., 15., 16., 17., 18., 19. and 20. Panzer Divisionen joining the line in time for the invasion of the Soviet Union in June 1941. By this time the initial mistakes in the organization of the Panzer division had been corrected as a result of battle experience, and this doubling of the number of divisions was made possible by halving the number of tank battalions in each. In 1939 the division had been too strong in tanks (theoretically, up to 320 light, medium and heavy tanks, serving in two mixed regiments totalling four battalions), and too weak in supporting infantry (two motorized battalions, plus a third on motorcycles). The division also had a two-battalion motorized artillery regiment, and single motorized reconnaissance, anti-tank and engineer battalions, together with support and service elements. Despite the quick German victory, tank losses in Poland were high – at least 218 were destroyed outright, and probably another 200 damaged beyond repair, totalling about 20 per cent of the total committed.

In 1940 the division's tank establishment was reduced to 230, and a second infantry regiment was substituted; but in the Western campaign, of just under 2,500 tanks available, more than 1,400 were still lightly armed, thinly armoured PzKw I and II types, and more than 300 were light PzKw 35(t) and 38(t) tanks taken over from occupied Czechoslovakia. In 1941 the divisional tank establishment was again reduced, to 190, in a single regiment of two (in a few cases, three) battalions; but by this time the numbers of medium (PzKw III) and heavy (PzKw IV) tanks were steadily increasing, and the light PzKw II was progressively limited to headquarters and reconnaissance units – although the Czech types were still in service in battle tank battalions of several divisions. Meanwhile the infantry component – now titled Panzergrenadiere – had been raised to two regiments totalling four battalions, of which the first in each regiment was (theoretically) equipped with armoured half-track personnel carriers, the rest still travelling in trucks; in practice there were almost never enough APCs to achieve that ratio. The artillery had been strengthened to three battalions, and a few of the guns were now mounted on self-propelled, armoured, tracked chassis rather than being towed; the same was true of some of the divisional anti-tank guns. (Note: before self-propelled equipment became available, a divisional anti-tank battalion was termed a Panzer Abwehr Abteilung; after they got tracked vehicles these units were termed Panzerjäger – literally 'tank-hunters', in Allied parlance 'tank destroyers'. The term 'Jagdpanzer' refers to some kinds of SP gun, not to a unit.)

The Russian Front between late 1941 and spring 1945 would prove to be a meatgrinder of armoured vehicles and their crews. After the initial easy victories of Operation 'Barbarossa' over the badly led Red Army formations with their outdated tanks, the Wehrmacht was increasingly confronted by the growing industry and apparently limitless manpower of the Soviet Union. Rebuilt after the costly setbacks inflicted by the Soviet counter-offensive in winter 1941/42 – which had seen them outclassed by the first of the new Russian T-34s – in summer 1942 the Panzers led the way across the Ukraine and deep into the south and east, reaching the Caucasus mountains and the fringes of the USSR's precious oilfields. But Hitler's obsession with capturing and holding the city of Stalingrad on the Volga, and the consequent frantic attempts to relieve the besieged Sixth Army, annihilated many German tank units. In February-March 1943 Field Marshal von Manstein won a great victory in southern Russia, but the USSR could make good its losses more easily than Germany.

Although a sideshow in terms of numbers, the British defeat of Rommel's Panzer Armee Afrika in October 1942 had already delivered a blow to morale; and only four months after the fall of Stalingrad the final Axis defeat at the hands of Anglo-American armies in Tunisia swept hundreds of thousands more German troops into captivity.

Besides the armoured divisions, the Wehrmacht also fielded a number of motorized, later mechanized infantry formations – the Panzergrenadier Divisionen. These had a single tank battalion to support two Panzergrenadier regiments – again, more often riding in trucks than in half-track APCs; an artillery regiment with towed and self-propelled guns, and strong reconnaissance, anti-tank and engineer elements. The tank battalion was soon replaced by one of tracked, armoured assault guns – Sturmgeschütze – which had made their first appearance in small numbers in France in 1940. Without revolving turrets, these were quicker and cheaper to produce, and from 1941 increasing numbers of Assault Gun Detachments (Abteilungen) and later Brigades (Brigaden) were soon reaching the front lines. Towed anti-tank guns, too, were slowly replaced with self-propelled guns mounted in German or captured tank chassis – the Tank Hunter Detachments (Panzerjäger Abteilungen). In the last two years of the war such units increased in number, to try to compensate for the dwindling numbers of tanks proper;

they often served as corps- or army-level assets as well as within Panzergrenadier divisions.

*   *   *

The spring thaw of 1943 following Manstein's victory in February had left the Red Army holding a deep salient thrusting into German lines around the town of Kursk in the southern Ukraine. In July 1943 Hitler ordered a vast offensive on two fronts to pinch off this salient; it failed, with the loss of hundreds of Panzers – including heavy PzKw VI Tigers and new PzKw V Panthers, of which so much had been hoped; thousands of hard-to-replace veteran crewmen died in this, the world's greatest ever tank battle. From mid-1943 onwards the Panzer divisions were essentially fighting on the defensive, rushed from sector to sector in the face of a succession of massive Soviet assaults. Their remaining strength was overstretched by the simultaneous need to fend off the Anglo-American armies in Italy and, from June 1944, the Allied invasion of France. The quality of their tanks remained high – the Panther was a world-beating design, and the massive 8.8cm gun mounted in the cumbersome Tiger was uniquely deadly; but there were never enough of them. The tank establishment of a Panzer division was reduced from 165 in 1943 to just a single battalion of 54 Panzers by the end of 1944; and during that year up-rated versions of the elderly PzKw IV still represented about half the tank strength of even the privileged and lavishly equipped Waffen-SS divisions, upon which so much of the burden now fell.

New Panzer divisions were formed, from young recruits mustered around the surviving remnants of wiped-out formations, or by converting other types of unit. The 21., 22., 23. and 24.Panzer Divisionen were raised in 1941, and the 25., 26. and 27. in 1942. The battle-proven 1., 2., 3., and 5. Waffen-SS divisions, originally motorized infantry, were progressively up-rated to Panzergrenadier and finally to Panzer status during 1942-44, and the Luftwaffe's elite 'Hermann Göring' Division followed the same path. In late 1943 the new 9., 10. and 12.SS-Panzer Divisionen were raised from scratch; and the Army's crack Lehr or demonstration units were also assembled into the Panzer Lehr Division, in time to face the Normandy landings the next spring. A number of other ad hoc, short-lived and usually chronically understrength formations were scraped together 'on paper' at the end of the war; but the main armoured and mechanized divisions to see combat during 1939–45 were as follows:

Panzer Divisions
Army:
1., 2., 3., 4., 5., 6., 7., 8., 9., 10., 11., 12., 13., 14., 15., 16., 17., 18., 19., 20., 21., 22., 23., 24., 25., 26., 27., 116., Panzer-Lehr (130.), 'Feldherrnhalle 1', 'Feldherrnhalle 2'
Luftwaffe:
'Hermann Göring'
Waffen-SS:
1.'Leibstandarte SS Adolf Hitler', 2.'Das Reich', 3.'Totenkopf', 5.'Wiking', 9.'Hohenstaufen', 10.'Frundsberg', 12.'Hitlerjugend'
Panzergrenadier Divisions
Army:
'Grossdeutschland', 3., 10., 14., 15., 16., 18., 20., 25., 29., 36., 60.'Feldherrnhalle', 90.
Waffen-SS:
4.'SS-Polizei', 11.'Nordland', 16.'Reichsführer-SS', 17.'Götz von Berlichingen', 18.'Horst Wessel', 23.'Nederland'

1. NATIONAL INSIGNIA

THE most universally applied marking used on German armoured vehicles was the national recognition sign. In its normal form this was a squared cross outlined in white, applied to both sides of tanks and other AFVs, and in some cases to the rear. This insignia was a natural development of the much more elongated so-called 'Greek cross' – *Balkenkreuz* – which in the closing year of World War I had replaced the 'Maltese cross' applied to German aircraft.

There were occasions when other, non-armoured vehicles also received this insignia, but the Wehrmacht regarded these as unofficial. A common instance was its use on captured enemy trucks and cars in forward areas. Such captures, which were very widely pressed into service by the Germans, were often painted with prominent crosses to avoid 'friendly fire' incidents; some photographs also show the swastika applied. Many of these added markings were crudely hand-painted.

Poland and the West

In its initial form, before the outbreak of war and during the Polish campaign of September 1939, the Balkenkreuz was in fact painted in solid white. When first ordered to be applied in August 1939 it was painted on the sides and rear of the turret, and in some cases also on the rear and front of the hull. However, once they reached the battlefields of Poland, vehicle crews soon felt that the white crosses were too prominent, and were providing too easy an aiming point for Polish anti-tank gunners even at longer than normal ranges. (A German report blamed perhaps 25 per cent of the total tank losses on this factor, although how it was possible to reach such an estimate seems puzzling.)

Above: September 1939: a Horch light personnel carrier leads an SdKfz 265 armoured command version of the PzKw I Ausf A along a Polish country road. Note the high visibility of the solid white Balkenkreuz painted on the front of the fixed superstructure.

The first expedient adopted was simply to paint out some of the white crosses, and to smear dark mud over the remaining insignia. A more lasting solution was found by painting them over – either completely, or leaving a narrow white border – with the deep yellow colour that was used for divisional insignia. Many units simply had the crosses painted out altogether, while others seem to have retained the full array.

Following the Polish campaign the development of an acceptable national marking continued, and by early 1940 designers had revealed a drawing of a symmetrically squared open cross similar to that used by the Luftwaffe. It was painted in white alone, i.e. as four L-shaped borders, with the centre to be left in the dark grey vehicle colour. Photographs from the brief Scandinavian operations of April 1940 show it marked on the sides and rear of tank hulls and the rear of the turret. Stencils and guidebooks were sent out to individual units, but in inadequate numbers, and in practice there were variations in application of the cross at unit level; some appeared with black centres, some with narrow black outer borders. However, by the time of the attacks in the West in May 1940 the majority of combat vehicles carried the correct style of Balkenkreuz, most usually on the hull sides only but with some use on the hull rear; the structural shapes of the various types of AFV dictated its placing to some extent. Wheeled armoured cars sometimes displayed

Below left: Spring 1940: during the Western campaign, British prisoners are carried on the rear engine deck of a PzKw I Ausf A. The rear hull shows the new style of Balkenkreuz, in white outline only on the dark grey paint finish.

Above: A park of PzKw I Ausf B and PzKw II tanks in 1939 show the solid white Balkenkreuz and tactical numbers on the sides and rear of the turrets. Within each Panzer battalion three of the companies had a mixture of light and PzKw III medium tanks, and the fourth the PzKw IV heavy tank.

additional crosses on the hull rear and front, including applications over radiator louvres.

The process of applying the national insignia was relatively straightforward. In most cases the border was traced on through a stencil and the rest was filled in by hand; some troops had access to sprayguns that sprayed directly through the stencil to produce the complete shape. Photographs show various sizes of cross in use; the most common size was that used on the PzKw III and PzKw IV, which was 25cm (roughly 10ins) high and wide.

North Africa

For this campaign, which begun for Germany in February 1941, another alteration to the Balkenkreuz was necessary. Against the sand-yellow camouflage paint applied to the vehicles of the Deutsches Afrika Korps (DAK) the white outline crosses were difficult to see. In a campaign involving three separate armies instant recognition was obviously even more necessary; consequently, the centre of the open white cross was filled in with black paint to improve the contrast. Again, there were many minor variations in shape and size, as well as in positioning on the vehicle. Among these variations were hand-painted crosses,

and narrow, elongated applications. Captured British vehicles had a variety of crosses painted on, often hastily; these were normally much larger than standard size and often applied over the entire cab side doors. Some were based on standard Balkenkreuz stencils with the arms extended; others were hand-painted, and differed considerably. While black crosses bordered with white were usual, some broad white crosses were seen applied to the tops and sides of vehicles.

The Eastern Front

For the invasion of the Soviet Union in June 1941, the task of stencilling and painting the 3,332 tanks, the hundreds of half-tracks and various other armoured vehicles, together with the many thousands of supporting trucks and cars – including many hundreds of French and some British captures – was an immense undertaking. Following the brief campaign in the Balkans that spring a number of armoured vehicles underwent a refit, and consequently were re-marked for the coming attack in the East. This led, once again, to a number of variations in the open white Balkenkreuz, with some captured vehicles receiving hand-painted crosses, and most being marked with oversized insignia. Although German troops and pilots had been given special enemy vehicle identification manuals, they were still unfamiliar with the Soviet types. In any case, it is seldom understood by troops on the ground that the often fairly subtle differences between one vehicle type and another are normally completely invisible to airmen flying at anything but the very lowest altitude and speed.

The invasion of the USSR was unleashed on 22 June 1941. The Panzers were still painted overall in the familiar dark grey factory finish, and until October of that year the Balkenkreuz generally remained unchanged; however, some variations were seen during the summer advances. These were due to vehicles being repainted and re-marked after damage repair or re-assignment to a new sector of the front. Among these variations were crosses with black outer borders; crosses in solid white with black borders; outline-only crosses in black or white; and crosses in unofficial colours.

Captured tanks

After the French capitulation in June 1940 significant numbers of French tanks of various Hotchkiss, Somua and Renault models were issued to German second-line units in the occupied countries, where they had some value for basic training and internal security duties. As the war progressed some went into action with units carrying out anti-partisan operations, particularly in the Balkans. These vehicles were prominently marked with German crosses, often in non-standard forms, e.g. narrow, elongated crosses in white outline on grey finish, and black outline on the 1943 dark yellow finish.

In Russia variations were again seen on captured vehicles, in the form of bold or oversized crosses. The first examples of captured Russian tanks pressed into service were seen with 1., 8. and 11. Panzer Division – during the summer of 1941. Although many considered it too dangerous to employ captured tanks, because most gunners fired on the silhouette rather than waiting to make out any markings, German units nonetheless risked it, trying to prevent such mistakes by painting large crosses or even swastikas on the turrets. Obviously, it was also standard practice to paint one of these symbols on the top of the turret in the hope

Above: Three PzKw I Ausf A tanks driving through a town; the nearest commander seems to wear a field-grey greatcoat over his black Panzer uniform complete with the large protective 'beret', dating this to winter 1939/40. The open white cross on the rear superstructure is the only visible marking.

of warning off Luftwaffe pilots. Despite the risks the use of such captures – particularly the excellent T-34 tanks – continued, though often limited to the infantry support role, where anti-tank recognition was not likely to be such a critical factor; they were also handed over to some of the Axis allied contingents.

(Photographs of German and Soviet AFV types bearing swastika markings may be misinterpreted: a large 'static' swastika with shortened 'feet' was the official national insignia of Finnish tanks operating alongside the Wehrmacht. This *hakaristi* was usually marked on the turret sides and hull front, in black with white 'shadowing'.)

Waffen-SS units also used captured tanks, and both 2.SS-PzDiv 'Das Reich' and 3.SS-PzDiv 'Totenkopf' are known to have pressed numbers of them into service. In March 1943, following bitter fighting to recapture the city of Kharkov, some 50 T-34s of various models fell into German hands more or less intact. These were repaired and modified to German standards, and repainted and re-marked. (Modifications included installation of the commander's cupolas from damaged PzKw IIIs and IVs, addition of *Schürzen* skirt armour plates, and fitting of items such as Notek lights, storage boxes, tools and radio equipment.) Twenty-five of these tanks entered service with a newly created III Abteilung (battalion) of 2.SS-PzRegt 'Das Reich'.

1942–45

In late 1941 Wehrmacht vehicles on the Eastern Front began receiving the first applications of whitewash snow camouflage, although this did not become the norm until the following winter of 1942/43 – largely due to the unavailability of suitable paint in 1941/42. Although identification of the vehicle was made harder, no actual modifications to the national insignia

Opposite: On manoeuvres in a training area in winter 1940/41, this PzKw I Ausf B bears the regulation open white stencilled cross. The obsolete PzKw I was retained for training purposes long after its withdrawal from combat units.

Above: Russia, autumn 1941: Panzergrenadiers hitch a lift along a churned-up road aboard a PzKw III displaying the standard open white Balkankreuz on its dirty grey finish. The Germans noted with alarm how the dirt roads vanished after only a few hours of rain; very few surfaced roads had been built in Western Russia, and even these quickly broke down under the weight of traffic now using them.

were ordered; however, some units chose to completely remove the Balkenkreuz during the winter, repainting it once the spring thaw arrived.

For nearly two years the open white Balkenkreuz remained relatively unchanged in appearance throughout the Wehrmacht. However, in February 1943 a new dark yellow factory paint scheme for AFVs was ordered, accompanied by the issue of green and brown for camouflage overpainting at unit level (*see* Chapter 7). For better contrast against this background, the black-centred Balkenkreuz was generally adopted for all vehicles; the sizes remained the same. In addition, some factory-applied markings on vehicles arriving in the front lines were non-standard. A good example is the Opel Maultier armoured half-track mounting the 15cm Panzerwerfer 42 rocket-launcher; these vehicles displayed a narrow, elongated cross with equal-width white and black bars, resembling the old 1918 aircraft marking.

Between December 1943 and September 1944 an anti-magnetic mine plaster preparation known as *Zimmerit* was applied to most tanks and assault guns in the field and to new vehicles leaving the factories. This thick, rough-textured coating made the application of the Balkenkreuz and other markings uneven in appearance.

For the remainder of the war no additional changes were ordered to the appearance or application of the Balkenkreuz, though many individual variations continued to be seen. These

even included white 'corners' either inside or outside black 'corners', with the centre left in background camouflage colours.

Air recognition flags

During the early years of the war, while the Luftwaffe enjoyed air supremacy over the battlefields, another type of national insignia was used, though never to the almost universal extent of the Balkenkreuz. This was the national flag – the black 'mobile' swastika on a white disc on a bright red rectangular field. The great difficulty of identifying vehicles from the air, either by their design or by the overall colour finish, has already been mentioned, and the problem had become apparent even during pre-war exercises. Mistakes caused Luftwaffe attacks on German columns during the Polish campaign, especially when crews began removing the early-type solid white crosses from their machines. The need for aerial recognition aids led to some units – in Poland, France, and North Africa – painting large white crosses, white bands or long rectangles, and in at least one case a large white swastika, on vehicle upper surfaces. However, a more helpful solution was the issue of large national flags to vehicle crews to be draped or attached over an available upper surface. This offered high visibility and colour contrast, and could be rolled out of the way in seconds when enemy aircraft were nearby.

The flag was in fact first seen during the Polish campaign, and by the operations in the West in May 1940 it was in extensive use. In North Africa the great similarity of the paint colours used by both sides, and the frequent use of captured vehicles, made it especially helpful. By the opening of the German invasion of the Soviet Union the national flag was almost universal issue, and remained so until mid-1942. At about that time, however, some German units advancing across the southern USSR in Operation 'Blue' became less inclined to display it: the Red Air Force now represented a growing threat, and losses to Soviet air-ground attack reached unprecedented levels. By late 1943, as the Russians and the Western Allies gained air superiority on virtually all fronts, the use of the national flag had become markedly less frequent.

Right: Summer 1942: two PzKw IIIs advance, with half-tracks and motorcycles in the background. The nearest tank shows a Balkenkreuz on the rear hull, possibly filled in with black; and note the large tactical numbers '535' painted on the turret rear bin, in red with white outlines.

Below: Summer 1942: mechanics from a maintenance company seem to be cannibalizing this badly damaged PzKw III Ausf J – a common practice. Although the grey finish is very faded by sun and dust, the contrast shows that the national cross has definitely been filled in with black. Above the head of the right-hand kneeling man the yellow inverted-Y divisional sign of 1.Pz Div can be made out; at this period this seems usually to have been displayed by command or lead vehicles, the others unofficially keeping the old oakleaf sign. The turret numbers '221' also seem to be painted in yellow.

Right: Although dating back to 1936, the PzKw III remained in production, in up-rated and up-gunned versions, into 1943. Judging by the peaked field-caps of the soldiers at right, that seems to be the date of this photo. Below the very large stowage locker that has been added above the engine deck, note the standard-size Balkenkreuz. The contrasting shades suggest that the tank is either still finished in grey, and the cross has been filled in black; or that the grey survives only in the centre of the cross, and the tank has been refinished in the new dark yellow ordered in February 1943.

Below: Autumn 1941 again, and infantry dismount from a PzKw 38(t) into the quagmire of the Roslavl highway. The standard Balkenkreuz is just visible on the side stowage bin.

Above: In summer 1941, these two PzKw IIs are being ferried across the River Dniepr; the open white national cross shows against the dark grey paint on the side stowage bin. Spare road wheels and track sections are carried on the nose, providing some extra protection to this thinly armoured light tank.

Right: France, 1940: this early variant StuG III displays a non-standard Balkenkreuz of very narrow, elongated form, recalling the old aircraft insignia used at the close of World War I. Although the standard cross was in general use by this date, such individual variations would continue to be seen throughout the war – sometimes due to the lack of proper stencils and instruction books. In some cases these narrow crosses had black central lines of the same width as the white borders.

Above: This PzKw 38(t) is
halted in a Russian street in
early autumn 1941. The
regulation national cross is
painted on the side bin, and on
the turret – as was normal on
this Czech type – very deep
tactical numbers in red outlined
with white – here, '401'.
Although it was normal for tank
crews to sling their steel helmets
(and in this case, their water
bottles) on the outside of the
turret to save space inside, the
helmets on the turret and nose
of this tank appear to be Soviet
souvenirs.

Right: This PzKw III
photographed in the sunshine of
early spring 1942 still has its
whitewash winter camouflage;
the Balkenkreuz on the side
shows dark grey with faint
white borders, but seems to
have a very thin coating of
whitewash. The soldiers posing
on it are not Germans but from
one of the Axis satellite armies –
judging by their caps and
tunics, possibly Finns.

Above: August 1942: a platoon of PzKw III Ausf J tanks crossing a German engineer bridge over the River Don during the drive towards Stalingrad. The national cross has been added to the hull rear stowage bin fixed to tank white '131' and, at the right, the yellow divisional sign of 24.Pz Div, which had been converted from 1.Kavallerie Div – a horseman leaping a fence, inside a broken circle.

Right: Early winter 1942: these two PzKw IVs have received full coats of whitewash camouflage, which even by this date was not universally available. The Balkenkreuz at the rear seems to have been filled in with black, although that on the hull side is probably in the original grey.

Right: Probably photographed during winter 1941/42, this assault gun battery commander's grey SdKfz 253 half-track leads whitewashed StuG III Ausf Bs past halted PzKw II tanks. The half-track displays a non-regulation Balkenkreuz, with narrow, elongated arms apparently filled in with narrow black lines. Note, right of the cross, the tactical marking 'Z1' in white.

Below: A late model PzKw III in action in the early winter of 1943/44 – note the standing soldier wearing the reversible, hooded winter over-jacket and trousers. Most of the skirt armour plates have been ripped off, but the remaining one shows a black and white national cross on the filthy dark yellow paint finish. The Roman 'II', painted on the turret spaced armour, apparently in black outlined with white, identifies a command tank of this Panzer regiment's 2nd Battalion headquarters (Stab).

Left: A rare photo of a PzKw IV Ausf A on the Eastern Front in summer 1942, displaying the standard open white cross on its grey finish. The PzKw IV, in close-support and up-gunned battle tank versions – and its basic chassis in many specialist conversions – was the most widely used German armoured fighting vehicle of the war.

Below: A brand new PzKw IV Ausf G rolls out of the factory in 1943. From the Ausf F2 which appeared in early 1942, the short 7.5cm L/24 howitzer for close support was replaced with this 7.5cm L/43 high velocity gun for tank-vs-tank combat. With the shift from grey to dark yellow factory paint finish from February 1943 onwards, the Balkenkreuz was filled in with black.

Left: Russia, 1943: a crewman passes a 7.5cm shell through the side doors in the 5mm spaced armour plate fitted around the turret of his PzKw IV Ausf H; the extra hull skirt plates are not fitted here. The black-and-white Balkenkreuz is now painted on the spaced turret plates. The tank is lightly camouflage-painted with green spots over the dark yellow finish.

Below: By 1943 the towed anti-tank guns of divisional Panzer Abwehr battalions were proving inadequate, and some were gradually replaced with self-propelled tank-destroyers using various German and captured tank chassis and guns. This Sdfz 131 Marder II mounts a 7.5cm Pak 40/2 AT gun on a PzKw II chassis. The black-and-white cross shows clearly against the dark yellow finish over-painted with dark brown camouflage.

Above: The need for self-propelled, fully tracked weapons to provide support for the tanks and infantry half-tracks also gave birth to this massive Panzerjäger 10.5cm K18 gun on the chassis of the PzKw IV – just one of many conversions using this basic hull, suspension and drive train. Photographed in 1942, it is still painted dark grey; note the small 'standard' size of the white national cross.

Left: Like the PzKw III and IV, late model StuG III self-propelled assault guns were also fitted with a longer, more powerful gun – a 7.5cm L/43 or L/48 – in place of the original short howitzer, and extra spaced armour skirts to explode shaped-charge projectiles before they hit the hull. This Ausf G, identifiable by the new commander's cupola, shows the toothed and angled side rails to which the skirts were attached. Note the open white Balkenkreuz, even though the two shades of camouflage paint behind the cross show that this vehicle has dark yellow factory finish. The rails around the engine deck are for fixing stowed gear – the lack of a rotating gun turret allowed StuGs to carry a lot of external stores.

Opposite top: Two artillerymen chat beside their snow-camouflaged StuG III Ausf G; the whitewash has been painted carefully up to the Balkenkreuz, leaving a little of the background colour.

Opposite: This dark yellow StuG III Ausf G photographed in summer 1943 lacks the skirt armour; a length of spare track has been fixed to the side, and the crew have painted a black-and-white Balkenkreuz over this.

Above: This early Tiger I Ausf E, fitted with the Feifel air cleaners on each side of the hull rear plate, may have been knocked out while serving with 2. Kompanie, sPz Abt 502 in north Russia in winter 1942/43. (The smoke candle dischargers on the turret cheeks were only fitted to tanks produced between August 1942 and June 1943.) It displays the standard size and placing of the Balkenkreuz for Tigers.

Right: A Tiger I during summer 1943, being serviced by one of the independent maintenance companies which kept the Tigers in fighting trim. On a background of dark yellow streaked with broad green and narrow brown lines, the standard national cross and the tactical number '122' are painted in black and white. Note also the interesting insignia on the maintenance truck at right, including 'St' for 'Stab' (HQ) in the rhombus sign indicating a tank company.

Above & right: Interesting photos from a sequence showing an early production Tiger I Ausf E being towed out of a marsh in summer 1943. Black '332', a tank of 3.Kompanie, sPz Abt 503, shows additional national crosses on the turret side and on each side of the number on the rear turret stowage bin. These seem to have been peculiar to this company of the battalion. (British private collection)

Right: Additional crosses were sometimes seen painted on the front and rear hull surfaces of armoured cars. Since these reconnaissance vehicles were more likely to find themselves in encounter battles at short range, it was particularly important that they be instantly recognizable. This line of SdKfz 222 four-wheeled cars were photographed at a railway station behind the front in June 1942.

Below: These T-34/85 tanks, captured by a Waffen-SS unit in August 1944, have not yet been re-marked, and for the moment only a swastika national flag on the turret roof shows their new ownership. Typically, they will receive a very large Balkenkreuz, narrowly outlined with black for maximum contrast, to the full depth of the turret sides. (British private collection)

Right: The nearest of these two PzKw V Panther Ausf D tanks displays a very small Balkenkreuz high on the turret; no other markings seem to be visible on either tank. Generally speaking, photographs of Panthers usually show them very sparsely marked.

Below: A rare photograph showing a knocked-out or abandoned Jagdtiger, whose 12.8cm gun was the heaviest mounted by any wartime AFV. Given its size – it stood more than 9ft high – the standard Balkenkreuz seems dwarfed. Note the very clear detail of the *Zimmerit* anti-magnetic mine plaster. Only 77 of these unwieldy 70-ton monsters were ever produced; some saw action in the West, with at least one Panzerjäger battalion (numbered 512). Slow, unmanoeuvrable, mechanically unreliable, fuel-thirsty and very hard to conceal, the Jagdtiger was a waste of scarce resources.

Above: Russia, summer 1941: during the first victorious advances of Operation 'Barbarossa', an early StuG III has just crossed a river on a bridge erected by engineers. A large national flag has been tied down over the stowage on the rear deck, as a recognition signal to the Luftwaffe who ruled the skies. During rapid advances it was particularly important for friendly aircraft to be able to identify the leading ground units, which might have covered miles since the pilots received their pre-flight briefings.

Left: In a similar scene, this PzKw III displays the national flag across the front of the turret roof.

Right: Being cloth, the national flag could be arranged over almost any surface or stowage load. This PzKw IV in summer 1941, towing a trailer of spare fuel drums, displays the flag tied down over a large stack of locally-cut timber beams attached to the rear deck for use if the tank needs 'unditching' from soft ground. Note the small white tactical number '331' on the rear of the turret. (British private collection)

Below: An SdKfz 251 half-track enters the city of Minsk in early July 1941. The national flag is hung from a rail rigged across the top rear of the hull; just above its upper edge, note part of a large, narrow Balkenkreuz painted centrally.

2. TACTICAL NUMBERS

D URING the creation of the Panzerwaffe in the 1930s the Germans gave individual number designators to each tank, for quick identification and control of individual vehicles by platoon (Zug) and company (Kompanie) commanders. Eventually almost the entire German armoured force came to use the numbering system to indicate a vehicle's position in a unit and sub-unit, such numbers being applied during the latter part of the war to many wheeled armoured cars, tracked personnel carriers and self-propelled assault guns and tank destroyers as well as to tanks.

The system of tactical numbers displayed on tanks took some time to evolve into a general practice, and exceptions to the usual rules would occasionally be seen throughout the war; unit and formation commanders could exercise their preferences, and front line conditions often governed the practicalities.

Unit organization

The Panzer brigade initially allocated to each 1939 Panzer division consisted of two tank regiments (Regimente), each of two battalions (Abteilungen). Each battalion consisted of a headquarters element (Stab), usually of four tanks; either two or three light/medium companies, and one heavy company. Each company had, in theory, a headquarters element with two tanks, and four platoons. Each light/medium company initially had two platoons each with between four and six PzKw I or PzKw II light tanks, and two platoons each with three PzKw III mediums; as more PzKw IIIs became available they gradually replaced the light types, at first forming mixed platoons. The heavy company's two platoons each had three PzKw IV fire support tanks. The companies within a regiment were numbered in sequence through both battalions, e.g. I Abteilung comprised 1. to 4.Kompanien, and II Abteilung, 5. to 8.Kompanien.

PzKw 38(t), probably photographed on the Eastern Front in summer 1941, and probably serving with the reinforced Pz Regt 25, 7.Pz Div. No fewer than 623 of these Czech tanks took part in the opening stages of Operation 'Barbarossa'. This regiment was known for its very large red turret numbers outlined in white, perhaps to ensure visibility on a type with which not all German gunners might be familiar. Here they are the '114' of 1.Kompanie, 1.Zug, tank No.4.

In practice, depending upon available vehicles and tactical doctrine, battalion commanders might reorganize their assets to give a better balance. Typically, one light/medium company might be stood down, its tanks being redistributed and its personnel forming a pool of spare crews; each of the remaining three companies had two light platoons, one medium platoon and one heavy platoon.

In 1941 most divisions had a single Panzer regiment of two battalions (though six of the regiments had three battalions). Most battalions had three companies – two of PzKw III mediums and one of PzKw IV heavies. In 1942 the last light PzKw Is and IIs were withdrawn; and slowly, as the first PzKw IV Ausf F2 and later models became available, with their long high velocity guns making the distinction between medium and heavy companies redundant, these progressively replaced the PzKw III in most units.

On the Russian Front during spring-summer 1942 resources were transferred from the quieter northern and central sectors to the more active southern sector; in the former areas many Panzer regiments were reduced to a single battalion, and in the latter regiments were increased to three battalions. It was also intended that each battalion should be raised once again to four companies, but this was seldom achieved in the face of the massive losses of 1942/43.

Above: PzKw I Ausf B photographed in summer 1939 before the Polish campaign, displaying the small rhomboid plate bearing the white number '103'. The radio aerial – which could be lowered from inside the tank by turning a handle, so as not to foul the revolving gun turret – confirms that this is a tank of a 1. Kompanie headquarters element. By no means all command tanks were of the Kleiner Panzerbefehlswagen conversion with a fixed superstructure, giving room for a three-man crew.

Left: PzKw I Ausf A on pre-war manoeuvres; despite the plate numbered '212' on the rear hull, identifying tank No.2 of 1.Zug, 2.Kompanie, this vehicle too has a radio fitted. Intended mainly for training, the PzKw I had a two-man crew, two 7.92mm MG13 machine guns, and 13mm armour all round – proof against small arms only.

From the second half of 1943 some lucky regiments began to receive the new PzKw V Panther to replace the PzKw IV in one of their two battalions, but this was never generally achieved. Indeed, in many units some companies or even a whole battalion might receive assault guns – with the main armament mounted for limited traverse and elevation in fixed superstructures – instead of tanks with revolving gun turrets. The official establishment of the 1944 Panzer regiment was two battalions each of three companies – I Abteilung with 1., 2. and 3.Kompanien, II Abteilung with 4., 5. and 6.Kompanien. Each company had two tanks in the HQ element, and three platoons each with up to five tanks.

Numbering systems

Various marking systems using one- and two-digit numbers were employed in pre-war training, painted on the turret sides and rear in large white digits. Single numbers might initially identify the individual tank; two-digit numbers appear to have identified the platoon first, followed by the tank.

Left & below: A PzKw I undergoing repairs during the summer of 1939. It was notoriously unreliable, and the Krupp-built Ausf A was always breaking down with overheated engine and brakes, and throwing tracks. This vehicle displays only a two-digit tactical number '10', probably identifying an individual tank of a training unit. The colour of the numbers may be deep yellow, which was not uncommon during training.

(1) PzKw I Ausf A, 5.Panzer Division; Poland, 1939
This division was part of Army Group South, which participated in the drive to Krakow. The tank is painted overall in dark grey RAL 7021 factory finish. The solid white *Balkenkreuz* has been painted on the side of the turret, and behind it the tactical number '522' for 5. Kompanie, 2. Zug, second tank.

(2) PzKw II Ausf C, 14.Panzer Division; Eastern Front, 1941
Some of the original dark grey RAL 7021 finish is still visible, but the tank has a weathered appearance, and the paintwork on the turret and superstructure is faded by sunlight and dust abrasion. Painted on the side stowage box is the white-outlined *Balkenkreuz*, which appears to have been re-stencilled by the crew to touch up discolouration and fading.

(3) PzKw 38(t), 10.Panzer Division; France, 1940
This Czechoslovakian-made tank has received a colour scheme of overall dark grey RAL 7021 with patches of dark green. The tactical number '632' has not been stencilled properly and parts of the white coat are missing or covered. The divisional sign of a yellow 'Y' with three dots has been crudely applied by hand in a non-standard position, and is over-sized.

(4) PzKw IV Ausf H, 20.Panzer Division; Eastern Front, 1943
This vehicle has had a coat of winter whitewash camouflage removed, and traces of it are still visible. The tank is now finished in a summer camouflage scheme of dark yellow RAL 7028 with oversprayed patches of olive-green RAL 6003. The tactical number '634' has been stencilled in white on the spaced armour plates around the turret. The divisional sign – a yellow arrow breaking through a barrier, giving the effect of wings – is painted on the side of the superstructure next to the driver's position.

(5) PzKw VI Tiger I Ausf E, schwere Panzer Abteilung 502; Eastern Front, 1943
This Tiger has a very rich camouflage colouring of RAL 8012 base paint (standard red-oxide primer), with dark yellow RAL 7028, olive-green RAL 6003 and red-brown RAL 8017 applied in a hard-edged pattern by brush. The single-digit white tactical number identifies the individual tank.

(Above) (6) PzKw V Panther Ausf G, 4.Panzer Division; Kurland, 1944
The summer camouflage scheme, of red-brown RAL 8017 and olive-green RAL 6003, is still partly visible under a liberal application of winter whitewash; on the turret the crew have brushed on the white in broad, wavy horizontal bands. All markings have been purposely removed.

(Below) (7) StuG III Ausf G of a Sturmgeschütz Brigade; Eastern Front, 1944
This vehicle displays a summer scheme of dark yellow RAL 7028 factory finish with overpainted bands of red-brown RAL 8017. Foliage has also been attached to the roof and wrapped round part of the barrel. By this date assault gun units were using three-digit tactical numbers like tanks, here '212'.

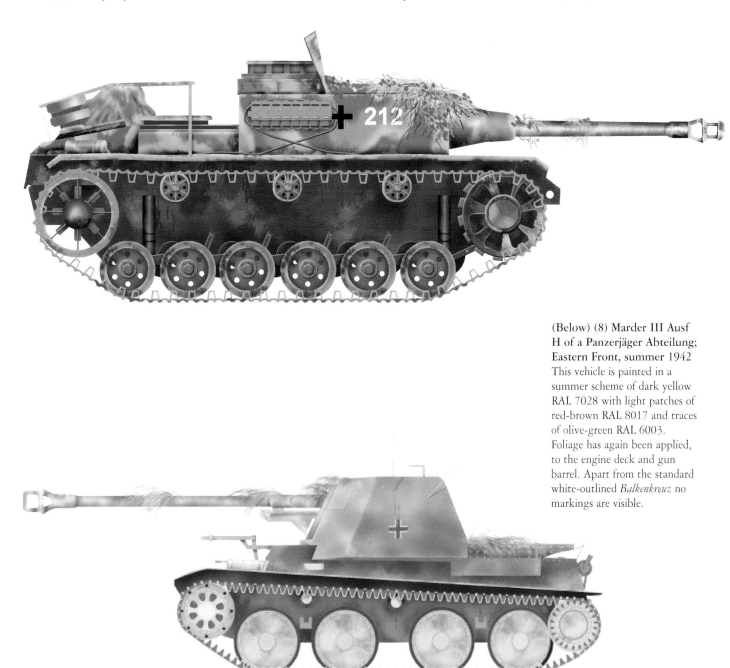

(Below) (8) Marder III Ausf H of a Panzerjäger Abteilung; Eastern Front, summer 1942
This vehicle is painted in a summer scheme of dark yellow RAL 7028 with light patches of red-brown RAL 8017 and traces of olive-green RAL 6003. Foliage has again been applied, to the engine deck and gun barrel. Apart from the standard white-outlined *Balkenkreuz* no markings are visible.

(Above) A PzKw IV Ausf D advancing along a Russian road in the summer of 1941, the overall dark grey RAL 7021 factory finish heavily powdered with pale dust. The *Balkenkreuz* has been stencil-painted on the superstructure side without first removing the radio antenna trough. The only visible marking is the three-digit tactical number on the rear of the turret box.

(Below) A PzKw IV Ausf E stationary in a field during the invasion of Russia, 1941; this tank bears the two-digit tactical number '18' in yellow on the turret sides and rear box. Since no platoon had eight tanks this cannot be a Zug-and-tank number, and its exact significance is unclear.

(Above) This Panther Ausf G has classic 1943–45 summer camouflage of dark yellow RAL 7028 with oversprayed patches of olive-green RAL 6003 and red-brown RAL 8017. The tactical number '121' is painted in red with white outlines, high on the turret side and off-set to the left of the turret rear.

(Below) This Nashorn 8.8cm heavy Panzerjäger photographed at a maintenance workshop – probably in Germany, 1944 – is finished in factory dark yellow with oversprayed patches of yellow-brown RAL 8000. Apart from the *Balkenkreuz* the only marking is the name 'Hornisse' stencilled in red above the louvres.

Splendid studies of crewmen posing in summer 1944 with a PzKw IV Ausf G command tank; note the *Zimmerit* plaster coating on the superstructure, and the spaced armour plates around the turret. The base coat of dark yellow RAL 7028 is oversprayed with patches of olive-green RAL 6003 and red-brown RAL 8017. The tactical number '508' has been crudely hand-painted in red-brown in two places on the turret plates; the standard two-colour *Balkenkreuz* has been applied on an uncamouflaged patch of dark yellow for better visibility. The frontal view shows that the turret front and mantlet have also received a non-regulation coat of *Zimmerit*.

The *Balkenkreuz* national insignia

(1) Poland 1939

(2) Variant, Poland 1939

(3) Standard 1940–42

(4) Variant 1940–45

(5) Standard 1943–45

(6) North Africa 1941–43

(7) Variant 1940–45

Waffen-SS Panzer-Division Markings

1. 1.SS.LAH – 1939–1940; 2. 1.SS.LAH – 1940; 3. 1.SS.LAH – 1941; 4. 1.SS.LAH – 1941–1942;
5. 1.SS.LAH – 1942; 6. 1.SS.LAH – Kursk Marking July 1943; 7. 1.SS.LAH – 1943–1945; 8. 2.SS.Das Reich –
1942–1945; 9. 2.SS.Das Reich – Kursk Marking July 1943; 10. 3.SS.Totenkopf – 1942–1945; 11. 3.SS.Totenkopf
– Kursk Marking July 1943; 12. 3.SS.Totenkopf – Kursk Marking July 1943; 13. 4.SS.Polizei – 1942–1944;
14. 5.SS.Wiking – 1941–1942; 15. 5.SS.Wiking – 1941–1942; 16. 5.SS.Wiking – 1942; 17. 5.SS.Wiking –
1943–1944; 18. 5.SS.Wiking – 1944–1945; 19. 7.SS.Prinz Eugen – 1941–1943; 20. 9.SS. Hohenstaufen – 1944;
21. 10.SS.Frundsberg – 1944; 22. 10.SS.Frundsberg – 1944; 23. 10.SS.Frundsberg – 1944; 24. 11.SS.Nordland –
1942; 25. 11.SS.Nordland – 1943–1945; 26. 12.SS.Hitlerjugend – 1944; 27. 16.SS.Reichsführer – 1943;
28. 16.SS.Reichsführer – 1944; 29. 17.SS.Gotz von Berlichingen – 1944; 30. 18.SS.Horst Wessel – 1944–1945;
31. 23.SS.Nederland – 1944; 32. 28.SS.Wallonien – 1944

Tiger Tank Battalion Markings

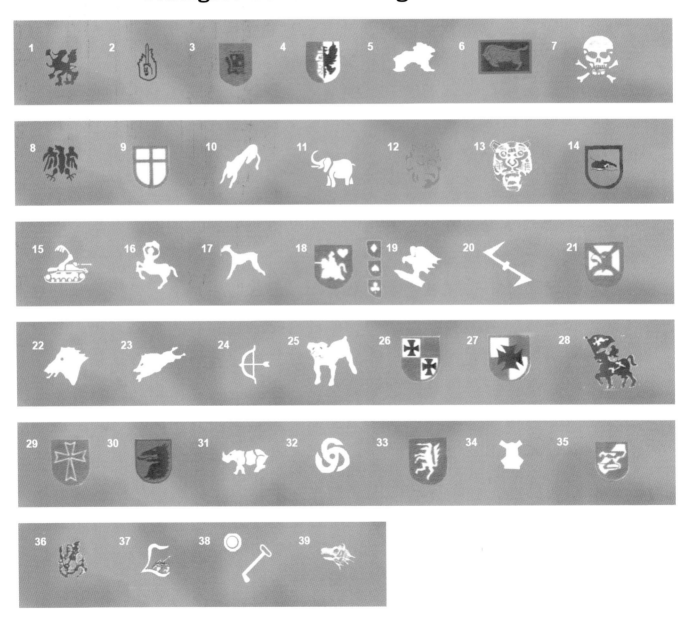

1. sPz.Abt.501; 2. sPz.Abt.502; 3. sPz.Abt.503; 4. sPz.Abt.504; 5. sPz.Abt.505; 6. sPz.Abt.506 [1944]; 7. sPz.Abt.506 [1943–1944]; 8. sPz.Abt.507; 9. sPz.Abt.508; 10. sPz.Abt.509

Sturmgeschütz Unit Markings 1940–1944

1. StuG.Abt.177; 2. AtuG.Abt.184; 3. StuG.Abt.185; 4. StuG.Abt.189; 5. StuG.Abt.190; 6. StuG.Abt.191; 7. StuG.Abt.192; 8. StuG.Abt.197; 9. StuG.Brg.201; 10. StuG.Brg.202; 11. StuG.Brg.203; 12. StuG.Brg.209; 13. StuG.Brg.210; 14. StuG.Brg.226; 15. StuG.Brg.232; 16. StuG.Brg.236; 17. StuG.Brg.237; 18. StuG.Brg.243; 19. StuG.Brg.245; 20. StuG.Brg.249; 21. StuG.Brg.259; 22. StuG.Brg.261; 23. StuG.Brg.277; 24. StuG.Brg.278; 25. StuG.Brg.279; 26. StuG.Brg.286; 27. StuG.Brg.287; 28. StuG.Brg.301; 29. StuG.Brg.322; 30. StuG.Brg.341; 31. StuG.Brg.393; 32. StuG.Brg.666; 33. StuG.Brg.667; 34. StuG.Brg.901; 35. StuG.Brg.912; 36. StuG.Brg.GD; 37. StuG.Brg.Panzer-Lehr; 38. & 39. StuG.Company.SS.LAH

Right: Light tanks on exercise in a forest in 1939; the leading vehicle, white '125', is a PzKw I, and white '131' is a PzKw II. These two types often served together in the same companies, in this case 2nd and 3rd Platoons of 1st Company; the PzKw II had a 2cm cannon as well as a machine gun, and its three-man crew was protected by 30mm frontal armour. The moderate size white numbers show up well against the dark grey paint scheme.

Left: Troops surround a halted PzKw 38(t) during operations in France in 1940; the large tactical number '522' on the turret rear is apparently red with white outlines. Nearly 230 examples of the PzKw 38(t) saw service in the West in 1940, mostly in 7. and 8. Panzer Divisionen. Note the stack of logs on brackets welded to the rear deck, for use under the tracks in boggy ground. Interestingly, none of the soldiers in this scene wears the black Panzer crew uniform.

Right: How PzKw 38(t) '441' toppled over is unexplained, but from the crater in the left background and the thrown left track it might have run over a mine? It was in France in 1940 that red turret numbers outlined white became widely used; exact styles varied, since units made their own stencils. The 38(t) mounted a Skoda 37mm AT gun that was powerful for its time; the tank was reliable, easy to maintain, and widely liked by its German crews.

During the Polish campaign the numbering was in transition to a three-digit system, and one-, two- and three-digit numbers are all (confusingly) seen in front line photographs. In September 1939 single digits seem to have referred only to the company, but two-digit numbers to the platoon followed by the tank. In three-digit numbers, the first identified the company, the second the platoon and the third the individual tank: e.g. '123' was the third tank of 2.Zug of 1.Kompanie. In 1940, when divisions still had two tank regiments, examples were seen of the three-digit numbers being underlined with a bar to identify the second regiment of the brigade.

This simple basic system continued in use throughout the war, but with frequent changes to accommodate changing tables of organization, and many individual variations and exceptions. Certain units employed different systems, e.g. with letters – 'A', 'B' and 'C' rather than a digit identifying the companies (*see* Chapter 5, 'Tiger Tank Units' for particular examples). Photographs also show PzKw II light tanks of divisional reconnaissance battalions bearing two-digit numbers prefixed 'A' for Aufklärungs. In most units the turret numbers seen within platoons and companies were seldom in consecutive sequences, or at least not for long after they left their depots in Germany and began the endless process of attrition and replacement; and in some units individual tank numbers were randomly allocated to platoons and companies from the start.

In c.1939–41 there were also some examples (e.g. in 1., 2. and 11. Panzer Divisionen during Operation 'Barbarossa') of a geometric shape being marked on tanks to identify the company (diamond, circle, triangle and square, for 1. to 4.Kompanien respectively), in association with two digits for the platoon and individual vehicle.

Command tanks

The digit '0' in the second position indicated a tank of the company command element: e.g. '201' identified the commanding officer of 2.Kompanie, '202' that of his deputy or 'AD'. In some units the two company command tanks were instead numbered e.g. '200' and '201'.

Tanks of the regiment's two battalion headquarters (Abteilung Stab) were usually identified by the Roman numerals 'I' and 'II' followed by '0' and a digit. The usual sequence was e.g. 'I01' for the battalion CO, 'I02' for his AD, 'I03' for the signals officer and 'I04' for the ordnance officer, and the numbers continued upwards on the light tanks of the battalion reconnaissance platoon. For those periods when regiments had three battalions, the same numbers appeared after the prefix 'III'. Regimental headquarters tanks were similarly numbered from 'R01' upwards. Only the first three of the Stab tanks were Befehlswagen fitted with extra command radio sets, and it was normal procedure for the AD to give up his tank to the commanding officer if the latter's tank broke down or was damaged.

Exceptions to this basic system were often photographed. In a few units the letters 'A' and 'B' identified battalion staffs instead of 'I' and 'II'. A commanding officer might use a properly marked tank at the beginning of a series of engagements, but battle damage or breakdowns would soon see him taking over whatever other vehicle was available. Some doubtless felt that using tanks with Stab indicators needlessly drew the attention of observant enemy gunners; and this danger was officially recognized from about 1943 and increasingly thereafter, when false numbering might be used instead of the 'R' designator. Since the normal division had only one tank regiment of two battalions with a maximum of four companies each, it was not uncommon to see regimental command tanks carrying numbers for a non-existent 9.Kompanie – '900' or '901' etc; and other regimental headquarters used numbers from '001' upwards. (Only a very few divisional tank regiments had temporarily on strength a company of Tiger tanks, numbered as 9.Kompanie, and in such cases regimental staff tanks might be marked '1001' upwards.)

Half-tracks, armoured cars and SP guns

In April 1944 an order was circulated changing the marking system in some respects. With effect from June, Panzer regimental and battalion HQ armoured vehicles *other than actual tanks* were now to display a two-digit number above '20', chosen at random, as the first part of a four-digit code. Three-digit numbers were also to be added to all half-track armoured carriers and

Left: Infantry support a PzKw 35 (t) as it goes into action against a concealed enemy position; this tank, displaying white '131' in the old smaller style digits, is almost certainly serving with 6.Pz Div in Russia, 1941. This would be the last campaign of the Czech types in German service, although they soldiered on with some of the Axis satellite armies.

Right: A PzKw II during operations in Poland in September 1939; the tactical number '211' is still painted small on the movable metal plate attached to the hull side. Throughout its active service career the PzKw II was under-armoured, and its turret ring was vulnerable to sustained machine-gun fire. Nevertheless, with 955 of them in front line service in May 1940 it was the most numerous type to see action in the Western campaign by a large margin.

Left: Three PzKw IIs of a battalion's 5.Kompanie on a training exercise in 1939. The nearest carries the tactical number '541', and the tank parked next to it the company commander's number '501', both on removable metal plates.

Right: A PzKw II bearing the large white tactical number '711', photographed after a training accident which sent it bulldozing through the wall of a substantial farmhouse or barn. The 2cm cannon and 7.92mm machine gun have been dismounted from the mantlet – this was standard procedure when the tank was parked overnight at the proving grounds.

wheeled armoured cars in Panzergrenadier, reconnaissance, assault artillery and other such units. No central records of numbering systems used within specific units and formations seem to survive, and these varied from division to division.

In tank destroyer units with early equipment such as the Panzerjäger I and the various models of Marder, no general numbering or lettering scheme is evident from photographs. Later, when the Panzerjäger received enclosed armoured vehicles such as the Panzerjäger IV, Jagdpanther and Hetzer, three-digit numbers became the norm (in 1943–45 this branch of service emphasized their kinship with the tank units in several ways). The two battalions of schwere Panzerjäger Regiment 656, equipped with the massive Elefant (Tiger P), used white three-digit numbers in a continuous sequence through its two battalions, Abt 653 (1. to 3.Kompanien) and 654 (4. to 6.Kompanien).

The assault gun battalions comprised a headquarters and three batteries, each of three troops, each of three guns, with a total of 31 guns; later these were redesignated from Sturmgeschütz Abteilungen to Sturmgeschütz Brigaden, and in 1944 their establishment was increased to 45 guns under the designation Sturmartillerie Brigaden. Initially the StuG IIIs seem to have displayed only a single letter to indicate the battery or troop, or alternatively a two-digit code identifying battery

and gun, e.g. '32' for second gun, 3. Batterie. Letter/number combinations were later seen; e.g. 'A11', presumably for first gun, first troop, first battery. However, StuG IIIs and IVs with three- or even four-digit numbers were also seen, the former from at least 1943 and the latter from 1944. The Sturmpanzer IV Brummbär was photographed carrying small numbers on the side, usually high up and behind a regulation or elongated Balkenkreuz – e.g. '1', '10', '46'; and in one instance, 'II', which is puzzling, since such guns are not thought to have been assembled in multi-battalion regiments.

Some self-propelled Panzerartillerie units initially used only battery letters, or alternatively individual names e.g. of cities or historical figures – two photographs show Hummel 15cm howitzers of Army and Waffen-SS units named respectively 'Koblenz' and 'Scharnhorst'. With increasing availability of SP guns it became usual for a regiment's I Abteilung to comprise 1. & 2. Batterie with the 10.5cm Wespe and 3.Batterie with the heavier Hummel; nevertheless, one photograph shows a Hummel confusingly marked 'A2' (perhaps for second gun, 3.Batterie unidentified, with the 'A' indicating I Abteilung?). Photographed Wespes show two-digit numbers – e.g. '43', '11' – presumably indicating troop (Zug) and gun number.

Left: Russia, summer 1941: two of the crewmen of a PzKw II Ausf F take their ease during a halt. The white outline turret number 'II07' may be filled in with red, or may be left in the background grey colour. This number places the tank with the Stab of its regiment's II Abteilung, in the reconnaissance platoon attached to this 2nd Battalion HQ. Note the position and proportions of the open white Balkenkreuz.

Application

In 1939 the three digits were most often displayed not on the tank itself but on removable thin metal plates, cut in the rhomboid shape of the map symbol for a tank company, and temporarily attached to the sides and rear of the vehicle. It was convenient to be able to shift them from one tank to another, but their small size made them invisible at much over a hundred yards – although they were often painted black as a high-contrast background to the small white digits. Those tanks which had already discarded these plates for the Polish campaign were re-marked with larger numbers painted on the turret sides and rear, usually in white but sometimes – especially after the accuracy of Polish AT gunners became clear – repainted in deep yellow, and often smaller.

Early in 1940 the removable plates largely disappeared from combat tank units in favour of larger painted-on numbers; some tanks at first carried both. These were applied to the turret sides and rear – or to rear stowage bins, where these were fitted. They were normally applied at unit level, outlined using stencils and filled in by hand, just as in the case of the national insignia, but photographs sometimes show what are certainly hand-painted numbers. These varied in neatness, consistency and alignment, from near-stencil perfection to later, sloppily daubed front line examples with copious paint drips below.

During the brief Scandinavian campaign of April 1940 numbers began to be painted in red with white outlines for higher visibility. In May–June 1940 tanks fighting in the Low Countries and France displayed both white and red/white numbering, some of them with three but some still with two-digit numbers, and occasional examples of the small rhomboid plates were still to be seen. By the invasion of the USSR in June 1941 three-digit red/white numbers were common, as they were in North Africa, but they were by no means universal. Plain white numbers were also retained, either solid or simply in outline on the dark grey finish, showing either two or three digits, and occasionally even single digits. As the war progressed some white-outlined numbers were filled in black, and some in other colours; these may have followed the Army's old bayonet-knot colour sequence for the companies within a battalion – respectively white, red, yellow, blue, and green for 1. to 3.Kompanien and Stab respectively. Obviously, interpreting colours other than black and white in most monochrome photographs can be little more than guesswork.

While styles, colours and sizes throughout the war show wide variation, the placing of numbers on the turret sides and rear remained the norm. There were instances, however, especially later in the war, of numbers being painted on the base housing of the gun barrel.

Left: Crews dismount to examine corpses beside the road as a column advances across the Soviet steppes. The nearest PzKw II carries a staff marking on the turret rear, rather obscured here but apparently the 'II05' of a tank of the II Abteilung reconnaissance platoon.

Right: The commander's use of the field-grey sidecap with his black Panzer vehicle uniform dates this PzKw II Ausf F to 1941 as well. The original three-digit number has been painted over and replaced at least once, and it now seems to be '741', in red or some other medium shade outlined with white.

Above: One of the very rare unposed front line photographs that look so perfectly composed that they might be movie stills. In summer 1941 a Russian village burns, while its former Red Army defenders come forward to surrender. The infantry MG34 squad are riding on a PzKw III numbered white '35' – tank No.5 of the 3rd Platoon of its unidentified company. Under magnification, the 'ghost' insignia of 11. Pz Div can just be made out on the superstructure side ahead of the Balkenkreuz.

Right: Another grey-painted PzKw III advances, past German infantry resting on a slope. The turret digits '143' appear to be in red with white outlines. A national flag for aerial identification is bundled up on the rear deck.

Left: Early 1941: the crews of these PzKw IIIs are showing off the finer points of their tanks to a group of unidentified troops. Note that the tactical numbers are still marked on small removable plates, suggesting that this photograph was taken in a training area in Germany.

Below: Libyan desert, 1942: a PzKw III has developed a mechanical fault and a crane truck from a maintenance company has come up to lift off the engine deck. The large tactical number '512' is painted on the rear of the turret stowage bin in red outlined with white. Just as on the grey finish used on the Eastern Front, this combination stood out more clearly than plain white on the yellow-brown desert paint scheme. The harsh sunlight and abrasive sand-laden winds of North Africa faded both background colour and markings rapidly; many photographs show repainted markings, sometimes relatively crude.

Left: An interesting view of a PzKw IV Ausf C displaying a three-digit tactical number on a plate temporarily attached to the nose. Display in this position or higher up the hull front was useful during training, but too visible for field use. Because each battalion's heavy company was the 4th, early PzKw IVs are usually seen marked with company numbers beginning with '4' or '8', and the second digit is normally '1' or '2'. This tank belongs to the Stab, 4.Kompanie, I Abteilung of its regiment.

Below: PzKw IVs photographed in spring or summer 1941 in either Yugoslavia or Russia. On the grey finish they display tactical numbers '727' and '626', apparently in white outline only. These indicate a regimental 2nd Battalion in which the 8th heavy company has been broken up and its PzKw IVs distributed to the platoons of the other three companies to provide a more balanced unit.

Above: Russia, 1941: a PzKw
IV Ausf E, covered in spares and
stores, is transported back to a
maintenance workshop on a
low-loader. Only the first '6' of
the tactical number can be
made out; the second digit,
painted over the turret side
door, seems to have been effaced
and repainted at some point.
Interestingly, the Balkenkreuz is
painted on a separate plate fixed
to the frame for spare road
wheels welded above the track
guard.

Right: This photograph
underlines, by comparison, the
major modifications needed to
keep the old PzKw IV in
combat service for so long.
Taken in Russia in early autumn
1944, it shows an Ausf H with
spaced turret and skirt armour,
the former showing a black or
dark red number '134' on the
dark yellow factory paint
scheme.

Right: The most conventional position for the tactical numbers on a StuG III assault gun: the '204' along the rear hull side seems to be in plain red on the dark yellow finish. The commander's cupola identifies this as an early production Ausf G, with a 'box' mantlet for the 7.5cm L/43 or L/48 gun. Note, behind the muzzle brake, no fewer than 18 white 'kill rings' for Soviet vehicles destroyed.

Below: A Red Army photograph of a destroyed early-model StuG III Ausf G, its roof plates blown off by the explosion of its stored ammunition. Note the concrete poured over the front superstructure to smooth over the shot-traps of the angled front plates. Here the tactical number '133', in red or black outlined with white, is painted on a separate plate fixed on top of the spare track links along the hull side.

Right: This StuG IV is re-ammunitioning from an SdKfz 252 half-track at some date after June 1944. It displays both its tactical number '332' and a Balkenkreuz on a separate metal plate wired to the stack of logs lashed along the hull side; the white-outlined numbers show up against a background of streaked camouflage painting. The half-track also has a tactical number – '324' – in accordance with the order of April 1944 extending three-digit numbering to most types of armoured vehicle.

Below: A knocked-out late-production StuG III on the Eastern Front, 1944. The tactical number '104' has been painted – apparently in white outline on a dark green or brown camouflage background – on the Saukopf ('sow's head') gun mantlet. This type of application was relatively rare; in this case it may have been for the sake of clarity, since the smooth steel of the mantlet is one of the few areas not covered with *Zimmerit*.

Above: An SdKfz 252 drives into a Yugoslavian town in April 1941. Note the contrast between the white of the elongated Balkenkreuz on the hull side at left, and the number '13' on the engine compartment, perhaps in deep yellow or red? The conventional mission of the SdKfz 252 was carrying spare ammunition for AFVs; since the crewman wears field-grey uniform we may guess that this vehicle might belong to a Sturmgeschütz Abteilung. At this date the tactical numbers were assigned at unit level, and there is no certain way of interpreting this example, though it may indicate the vehicle and battery.

Left: Russia, 1943: two SdKfz 251 armoured carriers, apparently from a Waffen-SS unit. The first half-track, which seems to have a coat of winter snow camouflage, shows a small, neat tactical number '813' in black on the nose plate, and to the right of this a faded '5'. The main number may perhaps identify the 8th Company within an unusually well-equipped regiment.

Above: Somewhere on the Eastern Front, one of the crew of a Panther PzKw V Ausf D2 poses on its powerful 7.5cm KwK L/70 gun. The application of *Zimmerit* dates this shot to after December 1943. The tank man's uniform insignia are unclear but seem to indicate an SS unit. The large tactical number 'A13' in red outlined with white is interesting; the letter may indicate either I Abteilung or 1.Kompanie of this unidentified regiment.

Left: Another Panther man caught by the camera, either working or resting on the tube housing the gun barrel cleaning rods. The 'drum' cupola and skirt armour again identify a PzKw V Ausf D2 in the East, mid 1943; the external smoke candle dischargers are rare in Panther photographs. The paint finish is dark yellow (RAL 7028) apparently with a very light streaked overspray of olive green (RAL 6003). The tactical number '245', in red outlined with white, is repeated to full size on the turret rear; it is more often seen smaller, at the upper left corner.

Left: Advancing along a dusty road on the Eastern Front, 1944, this Panther PzKw V Ausf A shows to advantage its full coat of chequer-pattern *Zimmerit*. The turret side number '212', repeated at the top left of the turret rear, appears to be in white thinly outlined with black.

Below: The multipole second radio antenna for an extra command set identifies this PzKw V Ausf G at a glance as a Panzerbefehlswagen. On the background of mottled camouflage paint the turret number 'I02', in white outlined in either black or red, further identifies it as the mount of the I Abteilung Stab deputy commander or 'AD'. Since only the first three tanks in the battalion headquarters have command radios, he will have to give it up to the battalion CO if the latter's Panther 'I01' is damaged.

Above: Tunisia, winter 1942/43: the crew of the much-photographed Tiger I Ausf E '141' of 1. Kompanie, schwere Panzer Abteilung 501 relax while a maintenance team try to fix one of the repeated engine malfunctions to which the 56-ton Tigers were prone. The overall colour of this first company of Tigers to reach North Africa is still discussed; modern research suggests that a coat of grey-green (RAL 7008) was applied over one of dark yellow (RAL 7028), producing a washed-out pea-green shade. The turret numbers are in white outline only; their large size was perhaps due to the Tiger being unfamiliar to Axis troops in Tunisia, who were also having to cope with recognition of previously unknown US vehicles at this date. Although hidden here by the stowed camo net, a peculiarity of sPz Abt 501 in Tunisia was a truncated Balkenkreuz, with short lateral arms but full height verticals.

Left: Tiger '122' of 1./sPz Abt 501, almost obscured by camouflage and stowage. Only 1. Kompanie repeated the turret numbers large on the rear stowage bin.

Above: Eastern Front, summer 1943: a Tiger I Ausf E of 2./sPz Abt 503 displays a more usual style of tactical numbering – probably '242' in black or red with white outlines. The overall paint scheme is dark yellow, which may have a very faint mottling in secondary colours. This company, in contrast to 3./sPz Abt 503 (*see* page 25), did not show extra national crosses, but the turret side numbers were no doubt repeated on the rear bin.

Right: This Tiger I on a rail flatcar in 1944 shows the turret number 'A22' in black – the letter over the *Zimmerit* plaster and the digits on a cleared patch of steel. The headquarters of both sPz Abt 507 and sPz Abt 508 used the 'A' prefix; but '22' seems too high a number for a Stab tank. The Tiger battalion of the elite 'Grossdeutschland' Div certainly used 'A', 'B' and 'C' company prefixes; and the presence on the next flatcar of a Panther also suggests that these are 'GD' tanks.

3. FORMATION & UNIT INSIGNIA

France, 1940: Pioneers preparing inflatable boats. The SdKz 251 has a large white air recognition panel painted on the upper rear hull; just below this can be seen the sign of 1.Panzer Division – an upright, outline oakleaf in white.

ALL ground combat divisions of the German Army, Luftwaffe and Waffen-SS were identified by a distinctive sign, which was marked on noticeboards, signposts and vehicles. These divisional signs were initially adopted for security and convenience, for quick recognition by the members of that and other formations without displaying the actual title. In time many of these signs became so well known to the enemy that any secrecy value was lost. It was for this reason that some of these signs were periodically changed, particularly before a major campaign or a redeployment – the best-known example being the new signs adopted by the Waffen-SS armour before the battle of Kursk in July 1943. Subsequently the division might revert to the original sign, or continue to use the new one. Quite apart from their value for security, or for quick recognition by German troops following signposts on the line of march, the signs proved to be good for morale – they were a visible focus of esprit de corps, with which the men of the division identified.

Even before the war a number of divisions had adopted such signs. Some of them were quite colourful, and were retained throughout the war; others were simplified so as to use only a single colour – black, white, red, blue, green or yellow. Regional or city coats-of-arms or other symbols of the area in which the division was raised were popular; others were traditional emblems drawn from history, folklore or mythology, or from the combat record of the division; others still were simple geometrical shapes and runic symbols. Before 1942 these signs were strictly controlled by the Armed Forces High Command (OKW), but in the second half of the war divisional commanders enjoyed much greater freedom, subject to approval to avoid duplication.

In a number of cases **individual units within divisions** also displayed their own signs – for instance, the bison of Panzer Regiment 7, within 10.Panzer Division – and these are noted in the divisional listing below. This could result in a number of signs being displayed simultaneously: for instance, a photograph of a motorcycle combination of a Luftwaffe unit attached to 11.Pz Div in the Balkans in 1941 shows the sidecar with the official 11.Pz Div sign on the top of the nose, the unofficial 'ghost' motif on the side, and the Luftwaffe unit's large circled elk-antler sign on the front.

Units were sometimes attached for significant periods to formations other than their parent divisions, and emphasized their identity by distinctive markings. For instance, after I/Pz Regt 6 was withdrawn from 3.Pz Div to receive the new PzKw V Panther tank it was rushed back to the front to serve with the Panzer Lehr Div, and marked its vehicles with a large white outline 'L' in place of the Lehr units' usual solid letter.

*   *   *

Photographs show that divisional signs were not widely used on vehicles during the 1939 Polish campaign; among a few exceptions were 1.Pz Div's white oakleaf emblem, and the three-pointed star of 4.Panzer Division. With the subsequent expansion of the Panzerwaffe many more signs were seen during the Western campaign of May–June 1940. New signs were allocated to some of the divisions which already had symbols, probably in an attempt to conceal their movements during the build-up for this Operation 'Yellow'. A number of others retained their older signs, or used both the old and new emblems in combination. For instance, some vehicles of 3.Pz Div on the Western Front used a yellow E-shape with the arms downwards (perhaps symbolizing the Brandenburg Gate in Berlin), while

Above: Russia, summer 1943: a PzKw IV Ausf H of Panzer Regiment 6 reverses under the cover of trees, guided by a dismounted crewman. On the turret spaced armour is the white tactical number 'I13' identifying a I Abteilung Stab tank; and beside it, the standing 'Berlin bear' sign of 3.Panzer Division, apparently also in white against the camouflaged background.

others displayed a yellow inverted-Y rune with two short vertical bars to the right of the top. The 4.Pz Div also had two symbols – the three-pointed star, and the circled 'man-rune'.

At the end of the campaign in the West the doubling of the number of armoured divisions in preparation for the offensive against the USSR was accompanied by an extension, and an attempt to standardize, the signs of the Panzer divisions. The majority of those allocated by OKW were progressive sequences of simple, vaguely 'runic' symbols. Some formations, not surprisingly, were reluctant to give up their old signs, and interpreted the regulations creatively: for instance, 1.Pz Div continued to carry the oakleaf emblem, while only some lead vehicles were marked with the new official yellow inverted Y. The regulation signs appear in most official Propaganda-kompanie photographs, but careful study of these and of private snapshots reveals a more varied picture. Such deviations from the rules were tolerated for the sake of morale, especially in the case of battle-hardened units that had earned respect.

In 1943–45, when the OKW allowed commanders to choose their own designs subject to a check against duplication, such duplications nevertheless did occur. For instance, both 3.Panzer and 293.Infanterie divisions sported the Berlin bear; and the 'sunwheel' swastikas of both 5.SS-Pz Div 'Wiking' and 11.SS-Pz Gren Div 'Nordland' were differenced only by an outline circle and shield background respectively.

Colour and placing

The divisional signs for the Panzer and Light divisions were normally applied in deep yellow, though both the background paint scheme and simple availability naturally led to some variations. For instance, 15.Pz Div used white, black or red signs on its desert-camouflaged vehicles in North Africa. When the factory paint scheme for AFVs changed from dark grey to dark yellow in early 1943 a number of previously yellow signs were changed to white. Throughout the war a total of about 40 emblems were painted in yellow in the Army Panzer divisions alone. Only three Waffen-SS divisions are known to have applied their signs in yellow at some point in their existence: 2.'Das Reich', 5.'Wiking' and 8.'Prinz Eugen' – the remainder used white. Among the Army Panzergrenadier divisions yellow was used for the signs of the 3., 10., 16., 18., 20., 60., and 'Feldherrnhalle'; the rest used white, black or red, alone or in combination.

No assault gun units are known to have used yellow for their insignia, which again were painted in white, black or red singly or in combinations. The Tiger tank battalions employed white and black, some signs being combined with yellow, red, and occasionally other shades. (See the colour pages for a selection of the signs of Waffen-SS divisions, Tiger battalions and Sturmgeschütz units.)

The placing of divisional signs was extremely varied, governed by the shape of the vehicle type, but was normally on the front and rear of the hull towards the left side; on the hull sides; or occasionally on the turret sides. It must be emphasized that very many AFVs did not display formation signs at all, particularly in the last year of the war.

ARMY PANZER DIVISIONS

For reasons of space not all the many changes in the incorporated combat units can be listed here. Those shown are relevant for the mid to late war years, with some early differences – before the reorganizations of 1940–41 – noted in brackets. In the first half of the war most Panzergrenadier Regimente were redesignated from former Schützen Regimente: the latter are only noted separately if they bore different numbers from the later Panzergrenadier units. Divisional units such as artillery regiments and reconnaissance (Aufklärungs) battalions were motorized before progressively receiving armoured equipment in 1942–44; some were simply redesignated with the prefix 'Panzer', but others, particularly some former motorized reconnaissance battalions, were also renumbered – only the definitive units are listed here.

1. Panzer Division
Formed: October 1935, Weimar
Insignia: 1939, white oakleaf; 1940–45, yellow inverted Y, but white oakleaf still widely used.
Main combat units: Panzer Regiment 1 (1939, plus Pz Regt 2), Panzergrenadier Regimente 1 & 113 (1939, Schützen Regt 1), Panzer Artillerie Regiment 73, Panzerjäger Abteilung 37, Panzer Aufklärungs Abteilung 1
Theatres of operation: Poland, 1939; Belgium & France, 1940; North & Central Russia, June 1941–February 1943; Balkans & Greece, 1943; Ukraine, November–December 1943; Central Russia & Poland, June–October 1944; Hungary & Austria, October 1944–May 1945.

2. Panzer Division
Formed: October 1935, Wurzburg
Insignia: 1939–40, two yellow discs side by side; 1941, yellow inverted Y with short vertical bar to the right of its top; mid 1943–1945, white trident.
Main combat units: Pz Regt 3 (1939, plus Pz Regt 4), Pz Gren Regte 2 & 304 (1939, Schtzn Regt 2), Pz Art Regt 74, Pz Jäg Abt 38, Pz Aufkl Abt 2
Theatres of operation: Poland, 1939; France, 1940; Balkans & Greece, 1941; Central Russia, 1941–44; France, 1944; Ardennes & W. Germany, 1944–45.

3. Panzer Division
Formed: October 1935, Berlin
Insignia: 1939–40, yellow E revolved to right, arms pointing down; 1941–45, yellow inverted Y with two short vertical bars to the right of its top; also, black rearing bear on ornate white shield. *Pz Regt 6* displayed on turrets the bear alone, in outline or solid white, red, yellow or blue; and from 1943, black round-bottomed shield bearing yellow *Yr*-rune above crossed swords.
Main combat units: Pz Regt 6 (1939, plus Pz Regt 5), Pz Gren Regte 3 & 394 (1939, Schtzn Regt 3), Pz Art Regt 75, Pz Jäg Abt 543, Pz Aufkl Abt 3
Theatres of operation: Poland, 1939; France, 1940; Central Russia, 1941–42; Southern Russia, 1943; Ukraine & Poland, 1944; Hungary & Austria, 1944–45.

4. Panzer Division
Formed: November 1938, Wurzburg
Insignia: 1939, yellow three-point star; 1940, yellow *Yr*-rune – Y with short vertical at top centre, within circle; 1941–45, yellow inverted Y with three short vertical bars to the right of its top.
Main combat units: Pz Regt 35 (1939, plus Pz Regt 6), Pz Gren Regte 12 & 33 (1939, Schtzn Regt 12), Pz Art Regt 103, Pz Jäg Abt 49, Pz Aufkl Abt 4
Theatres of operation: Poland, 1939; France, 1940; Central & Southern Russia, 1942–43; Latvia, 1944; Kurland & E. Prussia, 1945.

5. Panzer Division
Formed: Oppeln, November 1939
Insignia: 1940, yellow inverted Y with small disc to the right of its base; 1940–45, yellow X – latterly, on black background panel. *Pz Regt 31* used a lion insignia; and later, a red devil's head in half-profile on black background.
Main combat units: Pz Regt 31 (1939, plus Pz Regt 15), Pz Gren Regte 13 & 14, Pz Art Regt 116, Pz Jäg Abt 53, Pz Aufkl Abt 5
Theatres of operation: Poland, 1939; France, 1940; Yugoslavia & Greece, 1941; Central Russia, 1941–44; Latvia & Kurland, July–October 1944; E. Prussia, November 1944–1945.

6. Panzer Division
Formed: Wuppertal, October 1939, from 1.leichte Div
Insignia: 1940, yellow inverted Y with two small discs to the right of the centre; 1941–45, two yellow Xs side by side; during advance on Moscow, autumn 1941, yellow axe tilted half-left used as temporary sign.
Main combat units: Pz Regt 11 (1939–42, plus Pz Abt 65), Pz Gren Regte 4 & 114 (1939, Schtzn Regt 4), Pz Art Reg 76, Pz Jäg Abt 41, Pz Aufkl Abt 6

Right: France, 1940: a column of SdKfz 251s pass a stationary StuG III Ausf A. The leading half-track is a command vehicle, fitted with a platform above the driving position for map-reading. It displays on its left mudguard the 1.Pz Div oakleaf in white, above the tactical symbol for a motorized infantry platoon. On the right mudguard is a small '29', perhaps a vehicle number applied at unit level. The headlight cover bears the large white 'G' identifying divisions of the higher formation, Panzergruppe Guderian.

Theatres of operation: As 1st Light Div, Poland 1939; France, 1940; Northern & Central Russia, 1941–42; withdrawn to France, May 1942; Southern Russia, December 1942; Ukraine & Central Russia, 1943–44; Hungary & Austria, 1944–45.

7. Panzer Division
Formed: Weimar, October 1939, from 2.leichte Div
Insignia: 1940, yellow inverted Y with three small discs to the right of the centre; 1941–45, yellow Y.
Main combat units: Pz Regt 25, Pz Gren Regte 6 & 7, Pz Art Regt 78, Pz Jäg Abt 42, Pz Aufkl Abt 7
Theatres of operation: As 2nd Light Div, Poland 1939; France, 1940; Central Russia, 1941; withdrawn to France, May 1942; Southern Russia & Ukraine, February 1943–July 1944; Lithuania & Kurland, August–November 1944; E. Germany, 1945.

8. Panzer Division
Formed: Berlin, October 1939, from 3.leichte Div
Insignia: 1940, yellow Y with small disc to the right of the top; 1941–45, yellow Y with short vertical bar to the right of the base.
Main combat units: Pz Regt 10 (1939, plus Pz Abt 67), Pz Gren Regte 8 & 28, Pz Art Regt 80, Pz Jäg Abt 43, Pz Aufkl Abt 8
Theatres of operation: As 3rd Light Div, Poland 1939; Holland & France, 1940; Northern & Central Russia, 1941–44; Hungary & Czechoslovakia, December 1944–1945.

9. Panzer Division
Formed: January 1940, from 4.leichte Div

Insignia: 1940, yellow Y with two small discs to the right of its top; 1941–45, with two short vertical bars to the right of its base.
Main combat units: Pz Regt 33 (from March 1943, 'Prinz Eugen'), Pz Gren Regte 10 & 11, Pz Art Regt 102, Pz Jäg Abt 50, Pz Aufkl Abt 9
Theatres of operation: As 4th Light Div, Poland 1939; Holland, Belgium & France, 1940; Yugoslavia & Greece, 1941; Southern & Central Russia, 1941–44; withdrawn to France, March 1944; France, 1944; Ardennes & W. Germany, 1944–45.

10. Panzer Division
Formed: Stuttgart, April 1939
Insignia: 1940, yellow Y with three small discs to the right of its top; 1941–3, with three short vertical bars in that position. *Pz Regt 7* marked the silhouette of a bison on tank turrets.
Main combat units: Pz Regt 7 (1940, plus Pz Regt 8), Pz Gren Regte 69 & 86, Art Regt 90, Pz Jäg Abt 90, Pz Aufkl Abt 10
Theatres of operation: Poland, 1939; France, 1940; Central Russia, 1941–42; withdrawn to France, May 1942; Tunisia, December 1942–May 1943, when surrendered.

11. Panzer Division
Formed: Breslau, August 1940
Insignia: 1940–45, yellow circle bisected by vertical bar; also, white 'ghost' brandishing sword, on speeding tracks.
Main combat units: Pz Regt 15, Pz Gren Regte 110 & 111, Art Regt 119, Pz Jäg Abt 61, Pz Aufkl Abt 11
Theatres of operation: Yugoslavia, 1941; Southern & Central Russia, 1941–44; withdrawn to France, May 1944; France, 1944; Ardennes & W. Germany, 1944–45.

Above: Russia, 1941: although taken at night, this dramatic shot of the 7.5cm L/24 howitzer of a PzKw IV F1 firing allows us to make out, on the top left corner of its front superstructure plate, the new official 1.Pz Div sign of a yellow inverted Y. The white turret number '821' indicates No.1 tank, 2.Zug, 8.Kompanie in II Abt/Pz Regt 1.

Left: This PzKw III Ausf H, parading in Germany in 1941, shows (to the right of the driver's visor, as viewed) the sign of 2.Pz Div – the yellow inverted Y with a vertical bar to the right of it.

12. Panzer Division

Formed: Stettin, October 1940, from 2.Inf Div (mot)

Insignia: 1941–45, yellow Y in circle.

Main combat units: Pz Regt 29, Pz Gren Regte 5 & 25, Pz Art Reg 2, Pz Jäg Abt 2, Pz Aufkl Abt 12

Theatres of operation: Central & Northern Russia, 1941–43; Southern Russia, 1943; Northern Russia & Kurland, February 1944–1945.

13. Panzer Division

Formed: Vienna, October 1940, from 13.Inf Div (mot)

Insignia: 1940–45, yellow cross in circle.

Main combat units: Pz Regt 4, Pz Gren Regte 66 & 93, Pz Art Regt 13, Pz Jäg Abt 13, Pz Aufkl Abt 13

Theatres of operation: Southern Russia, 1941–44; Romania, 1944; Hungary, October 1944; destroyed at Budapest, January 1945. Remnant incorporated in Pz Div 'Feldherrnhalle 2' (qv).

14. Panzer Division

Formed: August 1940, from 4.Inf Div

Insignia: Yellow diamond with lower sides extended below to double length.

Main combat units: Pz Regt 36, Pz Gren Regte 103 & 108, Pz Art Regt 4, Pz Jäg Abt 4, Pz Aufkl Abt 14

Theatres of operation: Yugoslavia, 1941; Southern Russia, 1941–42; destroyed at Stalingrad, January 1943. Re-formed France, April 1943; Southern Russia & Romania, October 1943–July 1944; Kurland, October 1944–1945.

15. Panzer Division

Formed: November 1940, from 33.Inf Div

Insignia: Triangle bisected by longer vertical bar, usually in black, red or white. *Pz Regt 8* adopted a horizontal 'wolf-hook' (Wolfsangel) rune, normally in red. As part of the Deutsches Afrika Korps (DAK), all vehicles carried the white swastika-on-palm tree insignia of that formation.

Main combat units: Pz Regt 8, Pz Gren Regte 104 & 115, Art Regt 33, Pz Jäg Abt 33, Aufkl Abt 33

Theatres of operation: North Africa 1941–43; surrendered in Tunisia, May 1943. Remnant absorbed into 15.Pz Gren Div (qv).

16. Panzer Division

Formed: November 1940, from 16.Inf Div

Insignia: Yellow Y with horizontal crossbar; after division re-formed 1943, sometimes outlined black, possibly in commemoration of their dead at Stalingrad.

Main combat units: Pz Regt 2, Pz Gren Regte 64 & 79, Pz Art Regt 16, Pz Jäg Abt 16, Pz Aufkl Abt 16

Theatres of operation: Southern Russia 1941–42; destroyed at Stalingrad, January 1943. Re-formed France, May 1943; Italy, 1943; Ukraine, Poland & Czechoslovakia, December 1943–1945.

17. Panzer Division

Formed: October 1940, from 27.Inf Div

Insignia: Yellow Y with two horizontal crossbars.

Main combat units: Pz Regt 39, Pz Gren Regte 40 & 63, Pz Art Regt 27, Pz Jäg Abt 27, Pz Aufkl Abt 17

Theatres of operation: Central & Southern Russia, 1941–44; Poland, 1944; E. Germany, 1945.

18. Panzer Division

Formed: October 1940, from parts 4. & 14.Inf Div

Insignia: Yellow Y with three horizontal crossbars.

Main combat units: Pz Regt 18 (1940, plus Pz Regt 28), Pz Gren Regte 52 & 101 (1940, Schtzn Regte 51 & 101), Art Regt 18, Pz Jäg Abt 88, Pz Aufkl Abt 18

Theatres of operation: Central & Southern Russia, 1941–43; inactivated October 1943, and reorganized in Lithuania as 18. Artillerie Division.

19. Panzer Division

Formed: November 1940, from 19.Inf Div

Insignia: Yellow vertical 'wolf-hook' rune.

Major combat units: Pz Regt 27, Pz Gren Regte 73 & 74, Pz Art Regt 19, Pz Jäg Abt 19, Pz Aufkl Abt 19

Theatres of operation: Central & Southern Russia, Poland, 1941–44; E. Germany & Czechoslovakia, 1945.

20. Panzer Division

Formed: Erfurt, October 1940, from 19.Inf Div

Insignia: 1940–41, yellow E revolved to right, arms pointing down; 1942/43–45, yellow vertical arrow with downcurved 'wing' bars, sometimes shown as horizontal crossbar.

Major combat units: Pz Regt 21, Pz Gren Regte 59 & 112, Pz Art Regt 92, Pz Jäg Abt 92, Pz Aufkl Abt 20

Theatres of operation: Central Russia, 1941–44; Southern Russia & Romania, May–August 1944; E. Prussia & Hungary, 1944; Czechoslovakia, 1945.

21. Panzer Division

Formed: North Africa, February 1941, from 5.leichte Div

Insignia: White (N.Africa) or yellow (sometimes in France) D bisected by horizontal bar. As part of the DAK the white swastika-on-palm tree sign was also applied.

Main combat units: (N.Africa) Pz Regt 5, Pz Gren Regte 47 & 104 (1941, Schtzn Regte 104), Pz Art Regt 155, Pz Jäg Abt 39, Aufkl Abt 580. (France) Pz Regt 100, Pz Gren Regte 125 & 192, Pz Art Regt 155, Pz Jäg Abt 39, Pz Aufkl Abt 21

Theatres of operation: North Africa 1941–43; destroyed in Tunisia, May 1943. Re-formed France, July 1943; France, 1944; E. Prussia, E. Germany, 1945.

22. Panzer Division

Formed: France, September 1941

Insignia: Yellow arrow tilted half-right, with two crossbars.

Main combat units: Pz Regt 204, Pz Gren Regte 129 & 140, Art Regiment 140, Pz Jäg Abt 140, Aufkl Abt 140

Theatres of operation: Central & Southern Russia, February–December 1942; almost destroyed at Stalingrad, January 1943; remnants absorbed into 23.Pz Div (qv), April 1943.

23. Panzer Division

Formed: France, September 1941

Insignia: Yellow arrow tilted half-right, with one crossbar; and/or white silhouette of Eiffel Tower.

Main combat units: Pz Regt 23 (1941, Pz Regt 201), Pz Gren Regte 126 & 128, Pz Art Regt 128, Pz Jäg Abt 128, Pz Aufkl Abt 23

Theatres of operation: Central & Southern Russia, April 1942–1944; Romania, April–August 1944; Poland, September–October 1944; Hungary & Austria, November 1944–1945.

Above: Advancing victoriously into Russia in summer 1941, PzKw III Ausf Js pass an SdKfz 10; the yellow sign of 2.Pz Div can be seen on the half-track's mudguard. The SdKfz 10 was primarily designed to tow light guns such as the 2cm Flak cannon, 3.7cm and 5cm PaK 36 & 38 anti-tank guns, and the 7.5cm leIG 18 infantry howitzer.

Left: Byelorussia, July 1944 – and the passing of three years has brought a very different world for the Panzerwaffe. The whole front line of Heeresgruppe Mitte is about to crumble away under the hammer-blows of Operation 'Bagration', the Soviet summer offensive. In the path of this juggernaut is this PzKw IV Ausf H, its turret and hull sides protected by spaced armour plates, and its dark yellow paint scheme camouflaged with streaks of green and brown. Although the tactical number on the spaced plates cannot be made out, the white bear sign is still clearly visible. This would seem to identify 3.Pz Div – but see overleaf.

Above & right: An unusual opportunity to see both sides of the same tank – these pictures are perhaps stills from cine footage by a Propaganda-kompanie. They also present a considerable puzzle. This late-model PzKw IV seen during the Kursk offensive of summer 1943, white '420', quite clearly carries on its spaced turret plates the 'Berlin bear' always associated with 3.Pz Div; yet the photo above also shows, equally clearly, the yellow *Yr* or 'man-rune' of 4.Pz Div, left of the hull front machine gun. Note, in the divisional list in the text, that from 1943 the 3.Pz Div's Pz Regt 6 bore an extra marking – a black shield with the 4.Pz Div rune above crossed swords in yellow. This suggests that men transferred from 4. to 3.Pz Div were commemorating their old unit.

The colour of the bear is also uncertain; it seems to be a medium shade outlined white. Some sources say that it was painted in company colour-sequence – white, red, yellow or blue – which would make it blue on tank '420'.

Left: Russia, 1941: an example of the careful interpretation demanded by wartime photographs. This Panzer crew hurrying to clamber back inside their PzKw 38(t), marked yellow '122' on the hull side stowage box, have been identified elsewhere as belonging to 4.Pz Div, on the basis of the apparent 'man-rune' painted in yellow just left of the radio aerial base. In fact this is the circled-Y of 12.Pz Div, who had 107 of these Czech tanks for 'Barbarossa' – while 4.Pz Div had none.

24. Panzer Division
Formed: E. Prussia, November 1941, from 1.Kav Div
Insignia: Retained that of 1.Kav Div – white or yellow broken circle enclosing horseman leaping fence, right to left; 1943, re-formed division used simplified form, with rider replaced by diagonal bar.
Main combat units: Pz Regt 24, Pz Gren Regte 21 & 26, Pz Art Regt 89, Pz Jäg Abt 40, Pz Aufkl Abt 24
Theatres of operation: Southern Russia, June–December 1942; destroyed at Stalingrad, January 1943. Re-formed France; Italy, August–September 1943; Southern Russia & Romania, October 1943–August 1944; Poland, Hungary & Czechoslovakia, August 1944–January 1945; E. Prussia & Schleswig-Holstein, 1945.

25. Panzer Division
Formed: France and Norway, February 1942
Insignia: Red, round-bottomed shield bisected horizontally by a black bar; above this, three yellow stars; below it, yellow crescent moon points upwards – but there seems no photographic evidence for its application to vehicles. A simplified version showed, in yellow or white, three stars side by side, over a horizontal bar, over a modified crescent.
Main combat units: Pz Regt 9, Pz Gren Regte 146 & 147, Pz Art Regt 91, Pz Jäg Abt 87, Pz Aufkl Abt 87
Theatres of operation: Norway & Denmark, 1943; Central & Southern Russia, October 1943–May 1944; withdrawn to Denmark; Poland, E. Germany & Austria, September 1944–1945.

26. Panzer Division
Formed: France & Belgium, September 1942, from remnants 23.Inf Div
Insignia: 1943–45, Prussian grenadier's head in mitre cap, superimposed on smaller circle, all white.
Main combat units: Pz Regt 26, Pz Gren Regts 9 & 67, Pz Art Regt 93, Pz Jäg Abt 93, Pz Aufkl Abt 93
Theatre of operation: Italy, 1943–45.

27. Panzer Division
Formed: Voronezh, Southern Russia, October 1942
Insignia: Yellow arrow tilted half-right with three crossbars.
Main combat units: Pz Abt 127, Pz Gren Regt 140 (ex-22.Pz Div), Pz Art Regt 127, Pz Jäg Abt 127, Aufkl Abt 127
Theatre of operation: Southern Russia, 1942; disbanded, February 1943, and remnants absorbed by 7. & 24. Pz Divs (qv).

116. Panzer Division
Formed: France, March 1944, from remnants 116.Pz Gren Div
Insignia: Horizontal oval, enclosing greyhound – 'Windhund' – leaping from right to left over three tufts of grass on wavy ground line, all in white.
Main combat units: Pz Regt 16, Pz Gren Regte 60 & 156, Pz Art Regt 146, Pz Jäg Abt 226, Pz Aufkl Abt 116
Theatres of operation: France, 1944; Ardennes, 1944–45; Holland & W. Germany, 1945.

(130.) Panzer Lehr Division
Formed: Bergen & France, February 1944, from armoured training school demonstration (Lehr) units
Insignia: White script L. In 1944, II Abt/Pz Lehr Regt 130 marked PzKw IVs with a white square crossed by two equidistant diagonal red lines (high left, low right), or tilted diamond-wise on one point so the lines were horizontal. Unusually, the tank company tactical symbol – a small white open rhombus, sometimes with added company numbers – was seen marked front and rear on a number of tank hulls.
Main combat units: Pz Lehr Regt 130, Pz Gren Lehr Regte 901 & 902, Pz Art Regt 130, Pz Jäg Lehr Abt 130, Pz Aufkl Lehr Abt 130
Theatres of operation: France, 1944; Ardennes & W. Germany, 1944–45.

Panzer Division 'Feldherrnhalle 1'
Formed: November 1944, on paper, around remnants of 60.Pz

Above: A PzKw II rolling through a German town in winter 1939/40. Its tactical number '212' is painted in yellow on a rhomboid plate fixed below the radio antenna trough; the rather elongated Balkenkreuz is in black and white; to the right of this we see the yellow inverted-Y-and-dot of 5.Pz Div, which is also repeated at the right end of the front superstructure plate; and on the turret is the lion badge of Pz Regt 31, perhaps in red for 2.Kompanie.

Gren Div 'Feldherrnhalle' (qv); definitive title ordered March 1945
Insignia: Possibly as 60.Pz Gren Div? – two solid yellow Balkenkreuz one above the other; or possibly yellow vertical 'wolf-hook' rune.
Main combat units: Incomplete and uncertain; single un-numbered Pz, Pz Gren and Pz Art Regte, and Pz Jäg Abt, suffixed 'Feldherrnhalle 1'; Pz Regt possibly ex-Pz Bde 106; divisional units numbered 160
Theatre of operation: Uncertain – dispersed elements possibly in both W. Germany (Pz Abt 2106) and Hungary, March–April 1945.

Panzer Division 'Feldherrnhalle 2'
Formed: November 1944, on paper, around remnants of 13.Pz Div; definitive title ordered March 1945
Insignia: Possibly yellow vertical 'wolf-hook' rune.
Main combat units: Incomplete – units suffixed 'Feldherrnhalle 2': Pz Regt ex-Pz Regt 4, Pz Gren Regt ex-Pz Gren Regt 66, Pz Art Regt ex-Pz Art Regt 13, Pz Jäg Abt ex-Pz Jäg Abt 13, divisional units numbered 13
Theatre of operation: Hungary & Austria, March–April 1945.

PANZER UNITS IN ARMY PANZER GRENADIER DIVISIONS

Panzer Grenadier Division 'Grossdeutschland'
Formed: Pz Abt 'GD', April 1942; Pz Regt 'GD', January 1943 (one bn PzKw IVs, one bn Tigers; later one each PzKw IV, Panthers, Tigers).
Insignia: Solid white Stahlhelm, facing left.
Theatres of operation: Southern Russia & Ukraine, 1943–44; withdrawn to France; France, 1944; E. Prussia, November 1944–1945.

3. Panzer Grenadier Division
Formed: Pz Abt 103 joined division re-forming in France, spring 1944.
Insignia: Yellow vertical with two diagonal crossbars (low left/high right); sometimes in red.
Theatres of operation: Italy, June 1943–June 1944; France, August 1944; Aachen, November 1944; Ardennes, 1944–45; W. Germany, 1945 .

10. Panzer Grenadier Division
Formed: Pz Abt 110 joined division mid 1943.
Insignia: White upright key, teeth at top.
Theatres of operation: Southern Russia & Ukraine, autumn 1943–August 1944; Pz Abt disbanded after heavy casualties.

14. Panzer Grenadier Division
Details of Pz unit unknown; StuG and Pz Jäg Abt probably numbered 14.

Theatres of operation: Northern & Central Russia, Poland, E. Prussia, 1943–45.

Right: Here the Pz Regt 31 lion is painted on the rear of the cupola base of a PzKw IV. This regiment saw action in France in 1940 and the Balkans and central Russia in 1941, and it is hard to tell where and when this scene was recorded. However, note that the crewmen in the side doors both wear the Panzer beret, and the infantrymen still sport decals on the left side of their helmets; both these features point to a date in 1940 at the latest.

Below: Typical scene in the Russian autumn rains, as traffic ploughs along the rutted dirt road through a country village. At right is an SdKfz 223 leichter Panzerspähwagen (Fu) – a light armoured reconnaissance vehicle fitted with radio and a frame antenna. On its right mudguard (as viewed) is a tactical symbol; the yellow Y of 7.Pz Div; and a white pennant-on-a-pole sign, indicating a battalion headquarters sub-unit.

Left: Blurred but interesting photograph of a PzKw III halted during operations in Russia, winter 1941/42. The strangely elongated Balkenkreuz on the side box draws one's eye at once; but just visible above and ahead of it is the bison turret badge of 10.Pz Div's Pz Regt 7. This was made with a solid stencil held to the metal and sprayed around the edge with white paint, making an irregular nimbus around the dark grey image. A single-digit tactical number can be seen ahead of the bison, also in white outline and perhaps filled in with red paint which has since become very faded.

15. Panzer Grenadier Division

Formed: Panzer Abt 115 joined division in Italy, mid 1943.

Insignia: Black P on white five-point star.

Theatres of operation: Italy, September 1943–September 1944; Aachen, November 1944; Ardennes, 1944–45; Holland & W. Germany, 1945.

16. Panzer Grenadier Division

Formed: Pz Abt 116 joined division spring 1943.

Insignia: See under 116.Pz Div – but no oval frame round 'Windhund'.

Theatres of operation: Southern Russia & Ukraine, 1943 – thereafter see 116.Pz Div.

18. Panzer Grenadier Division

Formed: Pz Abt 118 joined division autumn 1942.

Insignia: Yellow V crossed by long horizontal bar.

Theatres of operation: Northern & Central Russia, 1942–44; E. Prussia, 1945.

20. Panzer Grenadier Division

Formed: Pz Abt 120 joined division autumn 1942.

Insignia: White square with five black 'dice' dots; transitional use 20.Inf Div (mot) sign – yellow anchor.

Theatres of operation: Northern, Southern & Central Russia, Poland, 1942–44; Berlin, 1945.

25. Panzer Grenadier Division

Formed: Pz Abt 125 joined division autumn 1942; Pz Bde 107, autumn 1944.

Insignia: Three horizontal antlers in outline shield, all white.

Theatres of operation: Southern & Central Russia, 1943–44; withdrawn to France; Metz, November 1944; W. Germany, 1944/45; Berlin, 1945.

29. Panzer Grenadier Division

Formed: Pz Abt 129 joined division in France, spring 1943.

Insignia: Unknown

Theatres of operation: Sicily, 1943; Italy, 1944–45.

36. Panzer Grenadier Division

Details of Pz unit of this short-lived division unknown; served at Kursk, July 1943, and remnants in retreat across Central Russia, 1943–44; re-formed as infantry division, May 1944.

60. Panzer Grenadier Division

Formed: Pz Abt 'Feldherrnhalle' joined division in France, summer 1943, when division and units granted that title.

Insignia: Yellow vertical 'wolf-hook' rune.

Theatres of operation: Central Russia, autumn 1943–summer 1944; Hungary, October 1944; almost destroyed at Budapest, January 1945.

90. Panzer Grenadier Division

Formed: Pz Abt 190 joined division after its formation in Sardinia and Corsica, June 1943.

Insignia: Diagonal bayonet (high left/low right) in Waffenfarbe colours – i.e. pink for Pz Abt – superimposed on white map of Sardinia.

Theatre of operation: Italy, late 1943–45.

Division 'Hermann Göring'

There is no space here for details of component units and operations as a Pz Gren formation before conversion to armoured division status.

Luftwaffe Panzer

Formed: France, October 1942, from Regt 'Hermann Göring'

Insignia: White disc 'clock face', each Pz company identified by position of black 'clock hand'; each Pz Gren company ditto plus white regimental number beside 4 o'clock position.

Main combat units: Pz Regt 'HG' (two Pz bns, one StuG bn), Pz Gren Regte 1 & 2 'HG' (three bns each), Pz Art Regt 'HG', Pz Flak Regt 'HG', Pz Aufkl Abt 'HG'

Theatres of operation: Sicily, 1943; Italy, 1943–44; Poland, July 1944; E. Prussia & E. Germany, October 1944–April 1945

Right: Heeresgruppe Mitte's drive into Russia in summer 1941: a column of PzKw 38(t) tanks from 7.Pz Div pass a halted line of the division's soft-skin vehicles. This provides an interesting example of two different signs used by one division: on the tank turret rear, right of the national cross, is the official yellow Y of 7.Panzer; and on the field car to the right we can see the white temporary marking also adopted.

Below: A Russian village burns in winter 1941/42, as grinning Panzergrenadiers from either Pz Gren Regt 110 or 111 return to their trucks. The right mudguard (as viewed) shows the white tactical symbol for motorized infantry and the platoon number '7', above the yellow divisional sign of 11.Pz Div – a circle bisected by a vertical bar. On the other mudguard in white are the vehicle number '15', and the 'Ghost Division's' unofficial badge, which was used at least as widely as the regulation sign. It showed a skeleton in a blowing cowl, waving a sword, with its feet on stylized tank tracks.

Above: An SdKfz 7 tows a disabled PzKpfw II over the timber bridge across a Russian stream during summer 1942. On the half-track's mudguard – and, under magnification, on the side of the tank – can be seen 24.Pz Div's sign, inherited from 1.Kavallerie Division. Note also the number '8' painted on the side of the half-track.

Left: This general's field car displays, on the left mudguard (as viewed), the white tactical sign of a command element. A tin command pennant mounted on the right fender is in the three colours of a divisional commander. On the mudguard above this is the Edelweiss sign of a Gebirgs (mountain) formation. The general wears the mountain troops' cap and sleeve badge, and the Ritterkreuz; he bears a strong resemblance to GenMaj Ferdinand Schörner, commanding 6.Geb Div in North Russia in 1941.

Opposite: In April 1941, just weeks before 'Barbarossa', Kleist's Panzergruppe had been diverted to invade Yugoslavia. His 11.Pz Div entered the capital, Belgrade, after only nine days. Here a StuG III is also marked with a 'J', presumably to identify the individual tenth gun (a StuG Abt had only nine two-gun platoons at this date). The PzKw IVs display white open squares on the rear of their turrets – the tactical marking for a battalion's 4.Kompanie. These geometric company shapes were seldom seen.

Above: The Horch field car, 'WH 556857', of GenObst Heinz Guderian, commanding Panzergruppe 2 on the central sector of the Eastern Front in summer 1941. With 850 tanks among his eight mobile divisions, Guderian slashed through the inept opposition to reach the Dniepr River in just 15 days. His Panzergruppe's vehicles were all supposed to display this bold white G. A grey rank pennant with a gold eagle and border is visible behind the headlight.

Below: This PzKw IV bears a white K on the trackguard, identifying Panzergruppe 1 commanded by GenObst Ewald von Kleist, Guderian's counterpart on the southern sector. With some 600 tanks, Kleist overcame numerical odds of about four to one against, breaking through and creating huge, doomed pockets of Soviet troops.

Above: This shot-battered PzKw III Ausf E command tank in North Africa displays, at the left of the front superstructure (as viewed), the white swastika-on-palm tree emblem of the Deutsches Afrika Korps. It seems to have been applied to the original dark grey finish, and left roughly outlined when yellow-brown (RAL 8000) was overpainted in a rough cross-hatched camouflage – which extends over the red-and-white turret number 'I01'.

Left: This PzKw II Ausf F of 21.Pz Div also bears a faded DAK emblem; much brighter is the white 'bisected D' of the divisional sign, seen here right of the driver's visor.

Opposite: Crewmen on a radio-equipped SdKfz 232 of Inf Regt (mot) 'Grossdeutschland'. The white Stahlhelm symbol predated expansion to divisional status in 1942. The tactical symbol is that of a signals platoon.

WAFFEN-SS PANZER DIVISIONS

1. SS-Panzer Division 'Leibstandarte-SS Adolf Hitler'
Formed: October 1943, from SS-Pz Gren Div 'LAH', whose SS-Pz Regt 1 had been formed summer 1942.
Insignia: All in white, diagonal key (low left/high right) in outline shield with clipped top right corner, later above two oakleaves. Kursk, July 1943, inverted white T.
Main combat units: SS-Pz Regt 1, SS-Pz Gren Regte 1 & 2, SS-Pz Art Regt 1, SS-StuG Abt 1, SS-Pz Jäg Abt 1, SS-Pz Aufkl Abt 1
Theatres of operation: Kharkov & Kursk, February/March & July 1943; withdrawn to Italy & Balkans, September–October; Southern Russia & Ukraine, December; withdrawn to France by April 1944; France, July–August; Ardennes, December; Hungary & Austria, January–May 1945.

2. SS-Panzer Division 'Das Reich'
Formed: October 1943, from SS-Pz Gren Div 'Das Reich', whose SS-Pz Regt 2 had been formed summer 1942.
Insignia: Yellow horizontal 'wolf-hook'. Kursk, July 1943, two white vertical bars on horizontal base bar.
Main combat units: SS-Pz Regt 2, SS-Pz Gren Regte 3 & 4, SS-Pz Art Regt 2, SS-StuG Abt 2, SS-Pz Jäg Abt 2, SS-Pz Aufkl Abt 2
Theatres of operation: Kharkov & Kursk, February/March & July 1943; Southern Russia & Ukraine, August-December; withdrawn to France by April 1944; France, July–August; Ardennes, December; Hungary, Austria & Czechoslovakia, January–May 1945.

3. SS-Panzer Division 'Totenkopf'
Formed: November 1943, from 3.SS-Pz Gren Div 'Totenkopf', whose SS-Pz Regt 3 had been formed winter 1942/43.
Insignia: White death's-head. Kursk, July 1943, three black vertical bars, or three white verticals on horizontal base bar.
Main combat units: SS-Pz Regt 3, SS-Pz Gren Regte 5 & 6, SS-Pz Art Regt 3, SS-StuG Abt 3, SS-Pz Jäg Abt 3, SS-Pz Aufkl Abt 3

Above: The Balkans, April 1941: an SdKfz 231 eight-wheeled armoured car, and an SdKfz 222 four-wheeler, both in dusty dark grey finish and displaying the early white key-in-a-pointed-shield sign of Inf Regt (mot) 'Leibstandarte-SS Adolf Hitler'.

Opposite: Fine study of an SdKfz 250/1 of the 'LAH' in 1943 or 1944. The licence plate has been censored, but the formation sign in its later form, with an oakleaf spray, is clear, apparently with a small '1' above it. So is the tactical symbol for II Abt Stab of a motorized infantry unit.

Theatres of operation: Kharkov & Kursk, February/March & July 1943; Southern Russia & Ukraine, August 1943–February 1944; Poland & Romania, March–October 1944; Hungary & Austria, January–May 1945.

5. SS-Panzer Division 'Wiking'
Formed: February 1944, from 5.SS-Pz Gren Div 'Wiking', whose SS-Pz Regt 5 had been formed winter 1942/43.
Insignia: Yellow or white circular 'sunwheel' swastika, sometimes on disc or within outline circle. Some use by tank regiment of white upright broadsword insignia centred on glacis.
Main combat units: SS-Pz Regt 5, SS-Pz Gren Regte 9 & 10, SS-Pz Art Regt 5, SS-StuG Abt 5, SS-Pz Jäg Abt 5, SS-Pz Aufkl Abt 5
Theatres of operation: Southern Russia & Ukraine, 1943; Cherkassy Pocket, January 1944; Central Russia, March–June; Poland, August–December; Hungary & Czechoslovkia, January–May 1945.

9. SS-Panzer Division 'Hohenstaufen'
Formed: October 1943
Insignia: White upright broadsword centred on H.
Main combat units: SS-Pz Regt 9, SS-Pz Gren Regte 19 & 20, SS-Pz Art Regt 9, SS-StuG Abt 9, SS-Pz Jäg Abt 9, SS-Pz Aufkl Abt 9

Theatres of operation: North Ukraine, March–April 1944; France, June–September; Arnhem, Holland, September; Ardennes, December 1944–January 1945; Hungary & Austria, March–May 1945.

10. SS-Panzer Division 'Frundsberg'
Formed: November 1943
Insignia: White Gothic F with tank company symbol as its crossbar, superimposed on diagonal oakleaf (low left/high right), within outline shield. Possibly also, block capital F within outline rhombus, various colours.
Main combat units: SS-Pz Regt 10, SS-Pz Gren Regte 21 & 22, SS-Pz Art Regt 10, SS-StuG Abt 10, SS-Pz Jäg Abt 10, SS-Pz Aufkl Abt 10
Theatres of operation: North Ukraine, April 1944; France, July–August; Arnhem, Holland, September; Rhineland, December 1944–January 1945; Pomerania & E. Germany, February–May 1945.

12. SS-Panzer Division 'Hitlerjugend'
Formed: October 1943
Insignia: White S-rune superimposed on diagonal key (teeth low left/handle high right), within outline shield, above oakleaf spray.
Main combat units: SS-Pz Regt 12, SS-Pz Gren Regte 225 & 26, SS-Pz Art Regt 12, SS-StuG Abt 12, SS-Pz Jäg Abt 12, SS-Pz Aufkl Abt 12
Theatres of operation: France, June–September 1944; Ardennes, December 1944–January 1945; Hungary & Austria, February–May 1945.

Armoured units in W-SS Panzer Grenadier Divisions

4. SS-Polizei Panzergrenadier Division
SS-Sturmgeschütz Abteilung 4; SS-Panzerjäger Abteilung 4

Insignia: All white. Until 1943, shallow rectangle with bottom bar extended each side; c.April 1943, an 'asterisk' – a cross and saltire superimposed; later, saltire and vertical bar superimposed; finally, large vertical 'wolf-hook' rune – Z with horizontal crossbar.

(**Note:** 7.SS-Frw Geb Div **'Prinz Eugen'** also had a leichte SS-Pz Kompanie, with captured French Hotchkiss H39 light tanks; and a StuG battery. *Insignia:* Yellow Odalrune within circle.)

11. SS-Pz Gren Div 'Nordland'
SS-Pz Abt (StuG) 11 'Hermann von Salza'; SS-Pz Jäg Abt 11
Insignia: 1942, white reversed N; from 1943, white or black vertical 'sunwheel' swastika within outline shield.

16. SS-Pz Gren Div 'Reichsführer-SS'
SS-Pz Abt 16; SS-Pz Jäg Abt 16 – both units equipped with Sturmgeschütz
Insignia: White or black double SS-runes, on box mantlet above gun barrel and on right of rear hull plate.

17. SS-Pz Gren Div 'Götz von Berlichingen'
SS-Pz Abt 17; SS-StuG Abt 17 (the latter redesignated SS Pz Jäg Abt 17 in June 1944) – both units equipped with Sturmgeschütz
Insignia: White armoured fist, diagonally (low left/high right) within outline shield, clipped at a top corner.

18. SS-Pz Gren Div 'Horst Wessel'
SS-Pz Abt 18 (equipped with Sturmgeschütz); SS-Pz Jäg Abt 18
Insignia: White SA-rune on thick circle.

23. SS-Frw Pz Gren Div 'Nederland'
SS-Pz Jäg Abt 23
Insignia: All white. Within outline shield with clipped top left corner, rune in shape of diamond with lower sides extended below to double length and terminating in arrowheads.

Left: The nearest of these Horch light personnel carriers displays virtually the same version of the 'LAH' sign as on page 67, but with a rounded rather than a pointed shield. At left is the symbol for a motorized infantry platoon. The white L-shapes are width markers, seen on many German vehicles.

Below: Muffled in their characteristic grey, fur-lined, hooded parkas, W-SS Panzergrenadiers ride a StuG III of 2.SS-Pz Div 'Das Reich' during the Kharkov fighting of early 1943. Note the yellow 'horizontal wolf-hook' rune divisional sign – like a reversed N with a centred vertical bar – just right of the Balkenkreuz.

Left: A rare formation sign – the white saltire-and-vertical used by 4.SS-Polizei Pz Gren Div in c.1943. The tactical symbol is hard to make out; it identifies one of a motorized regiment's headquarters elements, and may be that of a mapping team.

Below: An SdKfz 11 tows a 10.5cm leFH 18 howitzer along a dusty Russian road. The white 'sunwheel swastika' sign was used in only slightly different formats by both 5.SS-Pz Div 'Wiking' and 11.SS-Pz Gren Div 'Nordland', but this gun probably belongs to the former. The sign was also used by III (germanisches) SS-Pz Korps, to which both divisions belonged, but a light howitzer unit is not a typical corps-level asset.

Right & below: On display in a Soviet city, summer 1943, one of the many broken-down PzKw V Panther Ausf D tanks abandoned at Kursk in July. It belonged to the SS-Panther Brigade, a temporary unit assembled for this offensive. Finished in dark yellow with green camouflage streaks, the tank bears the red-and-white tactical number '521' on turret sides and rear. Ahead of the turret side numbers is an unusual example of a unit sign displayed on a PzKw V – this brigade's white panther's head with open jaws. (British private collection)

4. TACTICAL SYMBOLS

WEHRMACHT vehicles were all supposed to carry a composite set of tactical symbols, to identify exactly to which sub-unit within the unit and formation they were assigned. These tactical symbols were modifications of those used on German military maps for the types of vehicles and weapons that were deployed on the battlefield. After the earliest wartime campaigns it was unusual (though not unknown) for battle tanks to carry them, but they were widely seen on self-propelled guns, half-tracks and other AFVs. The Luftwaffe and Waffen-SS generally followed the standard practices of the Heer. Variations did appear – inevitably, given the complexity of the system and the numbers of units involved over several fronts and several years. However, these differences do not seem to have been systematic for any of the armed services; photographs do suggest that Waffen-SS units might have been more likely to mark tactical symbols on tanks, but as always, generalizations are unsafe.

The basic guide for troops was the booklet *Tactical Symbols of the Army*, available before the formation of the Panzer divisions, which was up-dated and amended in January 1943 to take account of changes in the tables of organization. Naturally, many examples of the older symbols continued to be seen.

The symbols were built up from several elements, combined to show the function or weapon of the unit; its class of vehicle; its size (i.e. whether a platoon or company, a battalion or regimental headquarters element, etc.); the sub-unit identity; and/or any special identification. Tables of these symbols have been published in many other books, and – given that few of them applied to AFVs – a complete guide here would be a misuse of

Above: France, 1940: captured French soldiers pass a line of SdKfz 251/1 Ausf B half-tracks halted at the roadside. This variant was the standard armoured personnel carrier for those Panzergrenadier units lucky enough to receive them; but in this case the white rhombus symbol painted on the left rear door, and the tarpaulin-shrouded loads, seem to indicate that they belong to a tank support unit of some kind – the small top element of the symbol, which would identify it exactly, cannot be made out.

space. The following brief explanation of some of the most relevant, together with the selection of photographs which follow, will be as much as most readers need.

Function/weapon: The basic symbol for artillery was a vertical line flanked by two shorter lines – a gun symbol, like a wheeled cannon seen from above – with additional details for function and class; towed units used the gun symbol below a line with a 'wheel' under each end. Tank units used a rhombus shape. Post-1942, when fully-tracked SP assault and anti-tank guns were becoming more available, such units also used the rhombus, with an arrowhead breaking the top line for Sturmgeschütz units and a T-shape (the anti-tank symbol) for Panzerjäger.

Type of vehicle: Other unit symbols – usually a simple 'box' – had at the base one 'wheel' for semi-motorized units, two for fully motorized, a wheel and an elipse for half-tracked, and (pre-1943) an elipse for fully-tracked, replaced by the rhombus thereafter. Motorcycle units used a circle enclosing a saltire, which was extended into a T-shape at the 2 o'clock position. Wheeled

Left & below: Probably photographed in western Russia during the early days of Operation 'Barbarossa', these motorcyclists' machines and sidecars do not carry the tactical symbol for a motorcycle battalion. The 'box' has a thick left edge and wheels at the base, and encloses an 'S', with '4' to the right – thus, 4th (Heavy Weapons) Motorized Company. Beside it within a frame is the script 'L' of Lehr units. This is far too early to be the Pz Lehr Div, only formed in 1944; so these men may belong to Lehr Brigade (mot) 900, which incorporated infantry and anti-tank units for the 1941 campaign.

armoured cars used a stylized left profile of the cab and bonnet of a car, above two, three or four wheels (for four-, six- or eight-wheeled vehicles).

Size, and identity: The left hand edge of the rhombus or box was supposed to be thick for a company, and not for a platoon. Headquarters vehicles had numerals or letters inside the box – e.g. St for Stab, I to III for battalions; and/or triangular pennant or square flag symbols above for battalion or regimental head-quarters. Sub-unit numbers were marked to the right of the symbol in Arabic numerals.

Special identity: Examples are e.g. the letters 'le' or 's' for 'light' or 'heavy', a thunderbolt symbol for signals units, a lance-with-pennant symbol (vertical line with single curved tick from top right) for reconnaissance units, etc.

Application

Symbols were usually applied in white paint, using a series of stencils to build up the necessary combination, by ordnance workshops before the vehicles were delivered to their units.

Those on vehicles that had been repainted, e.g. in new cam-ouflage colours, might be faint, roughly repainted, or simply absent. More effort was usually given to marking correctly those vehicles carrying ammunition, fuel, or maintenance crews; and such common softskin vehicles as field cars, which were allocated to almost every unit in a division and were thus liable to be misidentified (or filched), were usually properly marked.

On white snow camouflage symbols might be re-marked in black. There were some examples of units using the traditional seniority colour sequence – white, red, yellow, blue, light green, dark green – to differentiate companies or battalions.

Examples:

Panzer battalion HQ within two-regiment brigade (1939–40): Rhombus, enclosing e.g. 'II/1' for II Abt of senior regiment; on top, ball-and-streamer symbol over triangular pennant.

Panzergrenadier platoon, half-track APCs: Rectangular box; wheel and elipse under base; Arabic numeral to right.

Light SP Panzerjäger platoon (pre-1943): Gun symbol rising from two chevrons, above elipse; to left 'le', to right Arabic numeral.

Panzerjäger platoon (pre-1943): Right-angled triangle, base to left, hypotenuse upwards, above elipse; Arabic numeral to right.

Jagdpanzer battalion HQ (1943–45): Rhombus with T breaking top line, below triangular pennant.

SP Panzerjäger platoon, AT guns mounted on half-tracks (1943–45): Box, enclosing T; wheel and elipse under base; Arabic numeral to right.

Sturmgeschütz platoon (pre-1943): Gun symbol above elipse; Arabic numeral to right.

Independent Sturmgeschütz battery (1943–45) Rhombus, left side thicker; arrowhead breaking top line, small pennant below its barbs.

Armoured reconnaissance platoon equipped with half-tracks: Box; wheel and elipse under base; lance-and-pennant from top.

Tank maintenance platoon: Rhombus, enclosing eight-rayed sun.

Armoured supply company equipped with half-tracks: Box, left side thicker, enclosing saltire; wheel and elipse under base.

Above: Another characteristic scene from Operation 'Barbarossa': during a pause in the advance, a group of officers sit on a grass verge to confer over maps. Behind them an SdKfz 251 and a motorcycle combination both display the tactical symbol of a 'wheeled box' flanked by 'II', identifying the 2nd Battalion HQ of a motorized infantry regiment.

Left: Although indistinct, the symbols on the mudguard and sidecar of this combination can be recognized as the circled-saltire-and-extension of a motorcycle unit, with a sub-unit number to the right. The mudguard also bears the yellow circled-Y sign of 12.Pz Div; so these riders probably belong to Kradschützen Bataillon 22, that division's motorcycle infantry/ reconnaissance battalion in the early war years. The rapturous reception they are receiving probably places them in the Ukraine in 1941, when many civilians naively greeted the Wehrmacht as liberators from Stalin's despotic regime.

Above: During a ceremony at a Panzer training school in Germany in 1941, this PzKw 38(t) displays the unusual use of the rhombus tank company sign on the turret side. It is also reversed, with the thick leading edge to the right. The mark above it is unclear, but in this setting it may perhaps be the diamond shape sometimes used to identify 1.Kompanie? Note also, directly below the flag staff, the unusual placing of the large Balkenkreuz on the tank's exhaust shield.

Left: Summer 1941: Red Army prisoners straggle past Horch field cars, identified by the bold white G as belonging to Gen Guderian's Panzergruppe 2 with Heeresgruppe Mitte on the central sector of the front. This, together with the SS licence plate and the tactical symbol, strongly suggests vehicles of one of the motorized infantry regiments of SS-Div 'Reich' (the future 2.SS-Pz Div 'Das Reich'), which fought around Smolensk that summer. The 13.Kompanie of such regiments was the infantry gun company, with eight light howitzers.

Left: While repairs are made to this half-track, the left-hand front tyre and a section of rubber-faced track are stacked in front. On the mudguard (edged with a typical white L-shaped width reminder for guidance after dark) is a white tactical sign showing some typical variations of stencilling. The basic 'box' is that of a motorized platoon. The top edge shows a broken line, below a hard-to-see upper element. The diagonal division originally indicated cavalry units, but also – after 1942 – military police, and here the lower half is painted solid.

Left: A close-up of the mudguard of an SdKfz 263 eight-wheeled armoured car at a maintenance workshop somewhere in Germany, 1940. The tactical symbol is that of a reconnaissance platoon: the motorized unit 'box', with the lance-and-pennant symbol above, 'A' for Aufklärungs and the old cavalry diagonal division inside, and the platoon number '1' to the right. The SdKfz 263 was equipped with a long-range radio set, and was used primarily by signals and headquarters elements.

Left: An SdKfz 251 Ausf A during training in Germany, probably prior to the campaign in France in 1940. The half-track is sprayed overall dark grey, and the licence plate number shows pre-war allocation to Wehrkreis III (Berlin). The tactical sign for a reconnaissance platoon lacks the base element showing wheels or wheels-and-tracks. A wide range of softskin and armoured vehicles were used for reconnaissance, including some SdKfz 251s – although they were specifically designed as carriers for mechanized infantry, and were always in great demand for that role.

Below: An SdKfz 232 armoured car of the 'Leibstandarte-SS Adolf Hitler' motorized infantry regiment leads a column during the Polish campaign in September 1939. The solid white Balkenkreuz on the front plate (even painted over the tool handles) is typical of this date. The tactical marking denotes a motorized infantry unit; the special qualification 'Rc' is unidentified, but normally 'R' in this position indicated a regimental headquarters element.

Left: SdKfz 263 armoured radio cars on board railway flatbed trucks, destined for the front lines in southern Russia, summer 1941. For aerial recognition a national flag is flown on a pole. All these cars seem to fly two other flags, but these cannot be made out. Note the tactical symbol on the leading car's right nose plate, indicating a signals unit; immediately below this in a contrasting shade is a saltire cross – the yellow sign of 5.Panzer Division?

Below: A column of Deutsches Afrika Korps vehicles passing through Tripoli in Libya, 1941; a Horch field staff car leads an SdKfz 263 followed by two SdKfz 221 or 223 light armoured cars. The dark background to the DAK sign is grey paint left uncovered when the car was smeared all over with pale mud for lack of suitable camouflage paint – note the lumpy texture on the other wing. There the car displays the white tactical sign for a reconnaissance unit (*see* page 75), above what looks like a circled 'S', normally standing for 'schwere' – 'heavy'.

5. TIGER TANK UNITS

ITH a few exceptions noted below, most of the roughly 1,350 Pzw VI Ausf E Tiger I heavy tanks that were delivered to the Wehrmacht served not with divisional units but with separate Heavy Tank Detachments (schwere Panzer Abteilungen – sPz Abt) deployed at corps or army level. The commitment of these units to threatened sectors of the front lines could sometimes produce dramatic improvements in the local situation. Although its great weight (56 tons) made it difficult to move around areas which suffered from poor roads and weak bridges, the Tiger enjoyed a great advantage in firepower and survivability over most Allied tanks. When fighting on the defensive, especially in terrain offering plentiful cover, the Tiger's crews were able to make maximum use of the long range of its lethal 8.8cm gun, and the protection of its massive frontal armour. The psychological effect on Allied tankmen of knowing (or even suspecting) that they were advancing against Tigers multiplied the PzKw VI's combat value.

Because of the unique interest that this formidable tank still enjoys, the marking practices noted in photographs are listed here. It should not be supposed that these were general rules, however; as always, there were many variations in practice, and unit insignia were probably actually marked on tanks only in a minority of cases. These unit insignia are illustrated on the colour pages; when applied, they were usually seen on the left corner of the front superstructure and rear hull – other positions are noted individually below.

Apart from those delivered to Tunisia – which were painted dark yellow RAL 7028, some being overpainted with olive-green RAL 6003 or grey-green RAL 7008 – the overall paint finish followed that of other AFVS. Tigers delivered in winter 1942/43 were in dark grey RAL 7021; from February 1943 this was overpainted or replaced by dark yellow RAL 7028, with camouflage streaking and spotting in olive-green RAL 6003 and/or red-brown RAL 8017 being applied at unit level thereafter – individual photographs do not allow generalizations. Each winter the tanks camouflaged with whitewash; and for notes on *Zimmerit* plaster application, *see* Chapter 7.

Kursk salient, July 1943: as a Soviet-fortified village blazes, a Tiger I of one of the three Waffen-SS heavy tank companies seeks the next target. Coincidentally, each of the three companies lost only one Tiger during this massive battle. The spare track links and the crew's helmets and water bottles slung around the turret hide any tactical numbers which might identify the company. Note the national flag draped over the turret roof. The Feifel air cleaners at each rear corner of the engine compartment, and the big shrouds around the exhausts, make any display of markings on the hull rear difficult.

The tank is clearly finished in dark yellow paint, camouflaged with widely spaced streaks of – perhaps – red-brown; for what it is worth, this is the scheme illustrated in various sources for 13.(s)/ SS-Pz Reg 1 'Leibstandarte-SS Adolf Hitler' at Kursk.

Initially each heavy company's establishment was nine Tigers and ten PzKw III Ausf N; by the end of June 1943 this had been changed to 14 Tigers and no PzKw IIIs, giving the sPz Abt an establishment of 45 Tigers.

The insignia notes below apply only to the period when the unit had Tiger I Ausf E tanks, not the later Tiger II (Königstiger).

ARMY TIGER UNITS

schwere (Heeres) Panzer Abteilung 501
Received first Tigers: September 1942
Insignia: Stalking tiger, in yellow and black, black only, or white only – at least one tank carried this high on turret side. Insignia may only have been applied after surviving tanks of 1./ and 2./sPz Abt 501 were amalgamated with 7. & 8.Kompanien, PzRegt 7, 10.PzDiv and renumbered, in late February 1943. Some tanks also carried a white rhombus with a red left edge and script 'S' for 'schwere'. Large white outline three-digit turret

numbers, only repeated on rear in 2./sPz Abt 501. On joining 10.Pz Div, renumbered in red beginning '7—' and '8—'; e.g., '112' became first '812', then '712'.

Theatres of operation: Tunisia, November 1942–May 1943. Reformed unit to Eastern Front, November 1943; withdrawn July 1944 to re-equip with Tiger II (Königstiger); Poland, until disbanded, December 1944.

schwere Panzer Abteilung 502
Received first Tigers: August 1942
Insignia: White mammoth; initially painted large on turret rear (original turret bins fitted to left side). One- or two-digit turret numbers until spring 1943, thereafter three-digit, in white outline, solid black, solid white or yellow; e.g. large black '3' on snow camouflage re-marked as white '14' on dark yellow, finally as small white '113'. Tank of ace Lt Carius, at least 150 kills, bore small black '213'. Larger than normal Balkenkreuz, further back on hull sides than normal – this on black or dark grey panel after tanks repainted dark yellow.
Theatres of operation: Leningrad sector from late August 1942 (first operational Tiger unit); remained on Russian Front; redesignated sPz Abt 511, January 1945.

schwere Panzer Abteilung 503
Received first Tigers: November 1942
Insignia: Tiger head and neck, yellow and black. 3.Kompanie applied extra Balkenkreuz on turret sides and rear – *see* page 25.

Theatres of operation: Southern Russia, January 1943–April 1944; withdrawn to France; France, July–August 1944; September, withdrawn to re-equip with Tiger II; Hungary (redesignated sPz Abt 'Feldherrnhalle'), January 1945.

schwere Panzer Abteilung 504
Received first Tigers: February 1943
Insignia: Black outline rhombus enclosing diagonal spear (high left/low right) and tank track. In Tunisia, small plain red turret numbers. In Italy, 1944, some 1.Kompanie white turret numbers different sizes – large '1', outlined black; smaller, higher second and third digits, not outlined. Others, e.g. 2.Kompanie, single digits in white outline on turret sides and rear.
Theatres of operation: Stab and 1.Kompanie only, Tunisia, March–May 1943; 2.Kompanie, attached Division 'Hermann Göring', Sicily, July 1943. Re-formed unit, Italy, June 1944–May 1945.

Below: Russia, late 1943; the deputy company commander's Tiger of 1.Kompanie, III Abteilung, Panzer Regiment 'Grossdeutschland' – the 'GD' was the only Army division to have an integral Tiger battalion. The Stab still used turret numbers starting with the 'S' carried by the regiment's 13.Kompanie at Kursk; the other three companies now used 'A', 'B' and 'C' followed by two digits. The number seems to be in solid black on a dark yellow paint finish lightly mottled with a second colour. (British private collection)

schwere Panzer Abteilung 505

Received first Tigers: February 1943

Insignia: Initially, yellow snorting, charging bull. From early 1944, charging knight in black, both sides of turret; sometimes with plume and horse barding in company colour sequence – green for Stab, white, red and yellow for 1. to 3.Kompanien? Tactical numbers moved to base of gun barrel.

Theatres of operation: Central Russia, May 1943; Kursk, July; Southern and Central Russia, until July 1944, when survivors withdrawn to re-equip with Tiger II; East Prussia, September 1944–1945.

Opposite: Russia, summer 1944: battle-worn Tigers, covered with *Zimmerit* anti-magnetic mine plaster and roughly camouflaged in brown over dark yellow, cross a river. They belong to sPz Abt 506; the nearest is numbered '2', in 2.Kompanie's red outlined with white; the number of the furthest tank seems to be solid white '13', of 1.Kompanie. It is frustrating not to be able to see if they carry this battalion's handsome insignia painted large on the rear of the turret bin. (British private collection)

Below: During the run-up to the battle for Kharkov in March 1943, an SS-Hauptscharführer (senior NCO) tank commander of 8.(schwere) Kompanie, SS-Pz Regt 2 'Das Reich' shows off his massive mount to an Army officer. The shroud has been lifted off the left hand exhaust and put on the engine deck, allowing us to see the yellow 'wolf-hook' runic sign of this division, and a small Balkenkreuz (with very narrow white borders outlined in black) at the left end of the rear hull plate. (British private collection)

schwere Panzer Abteilung 506

Received first Tigers: August 1943

Insignia: Initially, white cross on yellow disc. Before end of 1943, yellow and black tiger with red mouth, holding red shield with white cross, all superimposed on large W, all outlined black, applied very large to rear of turret bin. The W – and single- and double-digit turret numbers – were painted in company colour sequence: green (Stab), white, red and yellow (1. to 3.Kompanien).

Theatres of operation: Southern & Central Russia, September 1943–August 1944; withdrawn to re-equip with Tiger II; Arnhem area, Holland, September 1944; Aachen, October; November, received 4.Kompanie; Ardennes, December; W. Germany, 1945.

schwere Panzer Abteilung 507

Received first Tigers: December 1943

Insignia: White blacksmith hammering sword on anvil, on white-bordered black shield, with cut-out at top right. Sometimes painted on rear of hull. Stab used letter 'A' and two-digit numbers; companies, three-digit numbers, the first large, the second and third smaller and lower.

Theatres of operation: Southern & Central Russia, March 1943–February 1945; withdrawn to re-equip with Tiger II; Czechoslovakia, April–May 1945.

schwere Panzer Abteilung 508

Received first Tigers: December 1943

Insignia: (Perhaps) black bison on black-bordered white shield. Stab/1.Kompanie used 'A' in place of first digit, perhaps others

Left: The crew, and one extra trooper, at work on the optics and weapons of the 'Das Reich' Tiger pictured on the previous page. The white snow camouflage has been painted neatly up to the edges of the turret number '832', which may be in either red or black. (British private collection)

Opposite: Two of the Tigers of the soon-to-be-renowned sSS-Pz Abt 101 moving up Route 316 to the front line near Morgny in Normandy, 7 July 1944. Note the heavy camouflage mottling of green and brown, and the *Zimmerit* cleared from a patch of steel to allow the neat application of the I SS-Panzer Korps insignia at the left (as viewed) end of the front plate. These are tanks from the legendary SS-Hauptsturmführer Michael Wittmann's 2.Kompanie; the nearest, with the turret number '223' in blue outlined with yellow, was commanded by SS-Oberscharführer Jurgen Brandt. Company commanders used any tank that was serviceable – on 7 July, Wittmann commanded from '205'; but in his famous battle at Villers-Bocage on 13 June he had used SS-Unterscharführer Kurt Sowa's '222', and when he was killed near Grandmesnil on 8 August he was in '007'.

'B' and 'C'? Tactical numbering varied, and sometimes applied on rear turret bin only. Examples of styles: 1.Kompanie, large white outline '1', second and third digits solid white, much smaller, lower; 3.Kompanie, single digits only, not on turret but hull side behind Balkenkreuz.
Theatres of operation: Italy (Anzio), January 1944; remained in Italy until February 1945; withdrawn to re-equip with Tiger II but personnel redistributed.

schwere Panzer Abteilung 509
Received first Tigers: September 1943
Insignia: Yellow and black tiger head in right profile, within black outline shield. Until summer 1944, large white three-digit tactical numbers in Cyrillic style.
Theatres of operation: Southern & Central Russia, November 1943–September 1944; withdrawn to re-equip with Tiger II; Hungary & Austria, January–May 1945.

schwere Panzer Abteilung 510
Received first Tigers: June 1944
Insignia: None known
Theatres of operation: Northern Russia, August 1944; E. Prussia & Kurland, late 1944–May 1945.

A few other 'scratch' Army Tiger units are recorded. A weak company known as **Tigergruppe Meyer** served with Pz Jäg Abt 46 in Italy in Augst-November 1943, lating fighting at Anzio in February 1944 under LXXVI Panzer Korps as **Tigergruppe Schwebbach**. Schwere Pz Abt 301 was formed in September 1944, fighting in the West during and after the Ardennes offensive; **sPz Kp 316** was attached to the Pz Lehr Div in Normandy in June–July 1944, and **sPz Kp Hummel** served at Arnhem in

September before being absorbed as 4.Kompanie by sPz Abt 506. Nothing is known of any insignia and marking practices.

13.Kp, later III Abt/ Pz Regt 'Grossdeutschland'
Formed January 1943; arrived Southern Russian front, March. July, 13. redesignated 9.Kp/Pz Regt 'GD'; fought at Kursk, turret numbers 'S' plus two digits. Expanded to III Abt, August 1942; the Stab and three companies used designators 'S', 'A', 'B' and 'C' respectively, followed by two digits. The battalion fought with the 'GD' on the Eastern Front until the final defeat.

WAFFEN-SS TIGER UNITS
Like the 'GD' unit, these were initially single companies attached to existing formations: 13.(s)/ SS-Pz Regt 1 'LAH'; 8.(s)Kp/ SS-Pz Regt 2 'Das Reich', and 9.(s)/ SS-Pz Regt 3 'Totenkopf'. One Tiger company was added to the Panzer regiment of each of these three premier SS-Pz Gren Divs with effect from November 1942. All three arrived on the Eastern Front in time to take part in the recapture of Kharkov in February–March 1943. Each company seems to have displayed the usual sign of its division.

For the battle of Kursk in July, they bore disguised divisional signs (*see* listing pages 66–67). Tactical numbers for the 'LAH' company were red with white outlines, large '13' followed by two smaller digits; for 'Das Reich', large white outline 'S' and two digits, some filled in red, and with a white 'imp' insignia ahead of them; and for 'Totenkopf', large three-digit numbers in black with white outlines. The 'LAH' company withdrew to Italy with the division following Kursk; the other two companies fought on in the East until spring and summer 1944. As their Tigers were used up and not replaced they were withdrawn and

their effectives were absorbed by the schwere SS-Panzer Abteilungen, below.

schwere SS-Panzer Abteilung 101
Formed: July 1943, Italy, partly from 13./ SS-Pz Regt 1 'LAH'
Insignia: That of the new I SS-Pz Korps: as 'LAH' Div but with two crossed keys. In Normandy, 1944, it is said to have marked turret numbers in blue, outlined yellow.
Theatres of operation: 1. & 2.Kp temporarily to Russia with 'LAH', October 1943–February 1944; battalion re-formed; France, June–August 1944; September, re-equipped with Tiger II, and redesignated sSS-Pz Abt 501; Ardennes, December 1944; Hungary, January 1945.

schwere SS-Panzer Abteilung 102
Formed: October 1943, partly from 8./SS-Pz Regt 2 'Das Reich'
Insignia: That of II SS-Pz Korps – S-rune rising from horizontal bar, reportedly in Panzer rose-pink. Seldom visible in photographs. Solid white turret numbers shown in diagonal row, forward digit low to rear digit high on both sides. Tiger ace Willy Fey achieved at least 69 kills in '134'.
Theatres of operation: France, July–September 1944; re-equipped with Tiger II, redesignated sSS-Pz Abt 502; E. Germany, February–May 1945.

schwere SS-Panzer Abteilung 103
Formed: November 1943
Insignia: None known
Theatres of operation: June–October 1944, training; Tigers repeatedly handed over to other units; October, re-equipped with Tiger II, and redesignated sSS-Pz Abt 503; E. Prussia, January–May 1945.

Below: Almost hidden by the foliage camouflage made necessary by Allied air supremacy, this Tiger being refuelled in Normandy is in fact '231' of 2./sSS-Pz Abt 102. Its commander, SS-Obersturmführer Loritz, was killed with all his crew near Ussy on 14 August 1944. The 'pink lightning' sign of II SS-Panzer Korps is not visible, and is only rarely seen in photographs of this unit's Tigers. (British private collection)

6. ASSAULT GUN UNITS

AS mentioned in the Introduction, the employment of most of the available tanks in mobile formations independent of the mass of the infantry became the ruling doctrine in the Wehrmacht before World War II. However, bitter experience in 1916–18 had proved that the infantry would suffer unacceptable casualties if they advanced against prepared defences without the support of mobile artillery to blast the machine gun posts and gun emplacements out of their path. If tanks were not to be dispersed among the attacking infantry to provide this support, it had to come from some other asset. Preliminary bombardment by conventional artillery and ground-attack by aircraft could do part of the job, but could not be counted upon to complete it.

While the Panzer debate was still going on, in 1935 Gen von Manstein proposed that each infantry division should be given a battalion of armoured, tracked assault artillery to provide this close support. These were part of the artillery rather than the Panzerwaffe, manned by artillerymen and organized in battalions each with a strong headquarters element and three batteries (companies) of three troops (platoons). In time the Sturmgeschütz or assault gun, with a 7.5cm howitzer or longer gun mounted in a low, fixed armoured superstructure on a fully-tracked tank chassis, became one of the most useful items in the German armoury. Infantry divisions never in fact received their own integral battalions, which were limited to Panzergrenadier divisions and a few of the most favoured Panzer divisions such as those of the Waffen-SS; most battalions – redesignated in 1944 as brigades, and given their own integral infantry company for protection – were assigned at corps level. However, as already mentioned, when the slowness of tank production became a major problem in the second half of the war the assault guns (and the similar but longer-ranged self-propelled Panzerjäger

anti-tank guns) were increasingly pressed into service in the Panzer divisions themselves to fill the gap. The distinction between the missions of the assault guns and the tank destroyers also became blurred – a fact famously reflected in the chaotic mix of insignia seen in some battalions.

The development of the assault guns was slow, and none were available in 1939. A few separate batteries each of six Sturmgeschütz III (StuG III) guns saw action in the West in 1940. Battery strength increased to nine guns, and complete Abteilungen (battalions) were reaching the front in 1941; eventually, about 70 battalions were in service, each with 31 guns. Their retitling as Sturmgeschütz Brigaden in 1943 was purely administrative; but in 1944 they were redesignated Sturmartillerie Brigaden, increased to 45 assault guns and howitzers plus an integral infantry company. (By no means all brigades were increased to this establishment by the end of the war, however.)

* * *

Throughout the war the tactical markings applied to the StuGs varied considerably. In 1940–41 some batteries displayed battery or troop letters, others various single- or two-digit numbering systems to identify the sub-unit and vehicle, and some bore individual names along with sub-unit designators. Many were seen, throughout the war, bearing the tactical symbols described in Chapter 4. Those few units assigned to divisions often displayed the divisional sign; but the majority of independent Abteilungen/Brigaden adopted their own signs, of which a selection are illustrated in the colour pages. These were painted on the front and rear superstructure or hull, or sometimes on the superstructure sides.

Opposite above: The death's-head insignia painted in white on a black panel on this StuG III Ausf A or B is the battalion sign of Heeres StuG Abt 192, seen here in action in 1941. Formed late in 1940 at the Juterbog artillery school, after costly fighting in Russia in 1941 this unit and the 16.(StuG) Kompanie of Inf Regt (mot) 'Grossdeutschland' were amalgamated into the assault gun battalion of 'GD', so the death's-head badge disappeared.

Above: More guns from StuG Abt 192; '34' is an Ausf C or D. The white numbers are painted in a distinctive 'Russian Cyrillic' style – a typical unit foible. The numbers seem to identify battery-and-gun, the first digits being 1 to 3, and the second 1 to 6 – at this date each of the three batteries had three troops each of two guns, a total of 18; the headquarters echelon had no guns and the commander used an SdKfz 250 half-track.

Right: This indistinct shot has two interesting features. The use of the field-grey version of the Panzer beret places the scene in France, 1940. 'F', apparently in yellow on the dark grey finish, must therefore identify 6.Zug, 3.Batterie.

Above: Infantry (probably Panzergrenadiere) are supported by a StuG III during operations in Russia in summer 1942. Without a revolving turret, the StuG was not only a much lower target (only 6ft 4ins high); the consequent lighter weight also meant that thicker frontal armour could be fitted than to early-model PzK III tanks. Its tank chassis made it capable of following the infantry into virtually any type of terrain to give close-up support. This assault gun carries only the letter 'A' in white; this may identify either the battery or troop, or the first gun in its sub-unit. The infantryman in the foreground has acquired a Soviet Tokarev SVT-38 semi-automatic rifle.

Below: Another blurred photograph that repays careful study. This StuG III, shown in Russia during winter 1941/42, is marked below the open roof hatch with the letters 'BF' in yellow on the worn grey paintwork. These are hard to interpret; they may perhaps indicate 2.Batterie (B), gun No.6 (F being the sixth letter of the alphabet).

Above: Troops hitch a ride on a StuG III crossing a shallow water obstacle somewhere in Russia, during either autumn 1941 or spring 1942. A large white 'B' is painted centrally on the rear hull, and far forward on the side of the superstructure.

Left: Heavy stowage – including a motorbike – hides the fine detail, but this gun photographed in winter 1944/45 is either a StuG III Ausf F or G with the long 7.5cm L/48 gun, or a rarer Sturmhaubitze 42 with a 10.5cm howitzer, as allocated to one troop of each battery of a 1944 brigade. The dark yellow finish is heavily mottled with brown and green camouflage, especially on the skirt plates. On the skirt and rear hull is a standard black-and-white Balkenkreuz. Centrally on the rear is a letter 'L', apparently painted in white outline with red infill. At the right end is the rhombus-and-arrow tactical symbol for a StuG unit, here enclosed in a separate frame.

Above & opposite above:
StuG IIIs crossing a
prefabricated bridge during a
summer movement in the
USSR; the dark yellow paint
scheme dates this to 1943, but
the lack of a raised
commander's cupola identifies
the guns to an earlier mark than
the Ausf G. A white open
Balkenkreuz is painted at the
left of the rear plate, and a unit
sign on the housing at the right.
This shows a dark cross on a
white shield, and may be that of
StuG Abt – from 1943, Brigade
– 201 (*see* colour section). Just
visible (above, opposite) is the
number '104' painted very
deep, and apparently in red
outlined with white, on the
superstructure side. From late
1942 assault guns began to be
seen with three-digit tactical
numbers.

Note too the very heavy loads
of stowage, including (above)
what looks like a complete spare
track, and spare road wheels.
The elements of the suspension
and drive train were always the
most vulnerable part of any
AFV, especially to mines.

Opposite: This early-model StuG III during Operation 'Barbarossa' displays, left of the open white Balkenkreuz just visible on the side, the sign of StuG Abt 243, a white knight on a red shield (see colour section). In the top right corner of the shield a white playing card symbol was added: a spade for the Stab, a heart for 1.Batterie (as here), a diamond for 2.Batterie and a club for 3.Batterie.

Right: Russia, 1942: apparently nervous about air activity, infantrymen shelter behind a StuG III (an instinctive move, but sometimes unwise – AFVs are high value targets, and draw enemy fire). The right rear trackguard carries the sign of an animal shape above the number '190', all in white within a white outline shield on the grey background paint. This use by StuG Abt 190 of an actual unit number is most unusual.

A column of StuG.IIIs rattle along a road, probably during the initial phase of the Balkans campaign, code-named 'Operation 25', in April 1941.

The assault gun is carrying a national flag, which can clearly be identified secured to the engine deck. No other markings can be seen on this vehicle.

Right: This photograph is included here mainly to emphasize the difference between the Sturm- or assault artillery, and the Panzerartillerie – self-propelled heavy howitzers in the indirect fire role, which were increasingly allocated to the 1st Battalion of the artillery regiment within the Panzer division. The latter's general marking practices are described in Chapter 2. This Hummel, mounting a 15cm howitzer on a PzKw IV chassis, is in Poland in summer 1944. It is not crewed by Panzer men – the dark figures wear fatigue clothing, but the three in the fighting compartment wear field-grey artillery vehicle uniforms of Panzer cut. Apart from the Balkenkreuz the only other marking on the softly mottled camouflage finish is a letter 'R' in white or pale yellow, which would normally identify vehicles under direct command of regimental headquarters.

Below: This Opel Maultier multi-purpose armoured half-track vehicle mounts a ten-tube 15cm Nebelwerfer 42 rocket-launcher, as part of the Panzerartillerie. The black 'B' on the side and rear presumably indicates the second vehicle or sub-unit. Note the very narrow, elongated Balkenkreuz on the side of the hull, apparently characteristic of Maultiers.

7. CAMOUFLAGE AND *ZIMMERIT*

LIKE all the other combatant powers, Germany had been obliged to pay serious attention to the whole subject of camouflage during World War I. It was during 1915–18 that for the first time very large opposing armies occupied virtually the same limited strip of terrain for months or even years at a time, under the constant scrutiny of the enemy and in danger from his massed artillery. This unprecedented episode of prolonged 'siege warfare' brought concealment – of men, guns, vehicles, positions, aircraft and ships – to a high level of both art and science.

In various contexts both the Entente and the Central Powers had explored the possibilities not only of hiding equipment by painting it overall with a drab, neutral shade to blend with its background, but also of breaking up the visual outline of things which could not be completely hidden, by using jagged, broken patterns of several colours. At first German equipment was painted in single shades, predominantly a matt grey; but as long-time world leaders in the dyeing industry, they also pioneered the manufacture of pre-camouflaged fabric to cover the wings of aircraft, printed in patterns of irregular, contrasting, multicoloured lozenges. The same principle of disruptive, multicoloured patterns was applied to the painting of trucks, artillery pieces and trench mortars – even the soldiers' steel helmets. When Germany was able to field a small tank force in the final year of the war multiple colours were employed. It was presumably felt that when parked up the enormous A7Vs would benefit from the same extensive use of camouflage netting and screens as all other static equipment; and that when in action, such a large, slow-moving mass of steel could never be concealed effectively against the devastated, almost treeless landscape of the war zone. In practice the A7V seems to have been finished in large or small patches of one or two camouflage colours – often brown and green – over a grey or ochre base coat.

At the end of World War I studies did demonstrate that camouflage had indeed been an important factor in limiting casualties overall and sustaining various units in the front line for long periods; and Germany continued to take an interest in such questions. During the early 1920s the small but intensely professional Reichswehr began to take steps to produce camouflage schemes of its own. In 1922 new standards for painting vehicles were issued, and those liable to be present on the battlefield itself were finished in a three-shade camouflage of dark grey, dark green and dark brown. The military soon established a programme to control the manufacture and application of camouflage paints; specifications were sent out to suppliers detailing the exact method of preparation, and the results were checked against colour swatches by inspectors at the vehicle assembly plants.

When Hitler came to power in 1933 and the unconcealed expansion of the new Wehrmacht was unleashed, the camouflage colours applied to military vehicles and equipment were changed. In 1935, the same year that the first Panzer divisions were formed, a new standardized camouflage scheme for all vehicles and large equipment items was ordered, in two colours – dark grey and dark brown. The vehicles and equipment were painted in random patterns of round-edged patches, one-third of the total surface to show dark brown and two-thirds dark grey. The specific colours were allocated shade numbers in the RAL series – sometimes retrospectively – which will be used throughout this text to avoid confusion. The dark grey (which in future would be codified as RAL 7021) and dark brown (at that date specified as No.45) were darker than the three shades formerly used, since it was believed that vehicles and other major items of equipment were likely to be parked in the shadows cast by buildings, trees or field boundaries. Experience during training manoeuvres suggested that with a little use sunlight, dust and mud soon softened the contrast between the grey and brown areas, and helped vehicles merge naturally with the colours of the terrain in which they were operating.

Europe & Russia, 1939–42

A further change was ordered late in 1939, abandoning the dark brown in favour of overall dark grey RAL 7021 – apparently for reasons of economy and speed at a time of hasty enlargement of the Wehrmacht. Not surprisingly, a proportion of the vehicles committed in Poland that September were still finished in the two-tone camouflage. During winter 1939/spring 1940 new vehicles left the factory finished grey overall, and vehicles in service or under repair were repainted to match. The great majority of vehicles deployed for the May 1940 campaign in the West were overall grey, and this was finally standardized by an order of 31 July that year.

Opposite: A PzKw I shows a clear view of the dark grey and brown camouflage pattern adopted in 1935. The lack of the national insignia (eagle and swastika) on the commander's black beret dates this to before November that year.

Above: Two PzKw I Ausf As on a training exercise, summer 1939. No markings are visible, but they are clearly still camouflaged in dark grey with dark brown No.45 blotches. The PzKw I had only a two-man crew: the driver, and the commander/gunner/loader (and radioman, if it was a command tank). More than 1,500 of these little 5.8-ton vehicles were available at the start of the Polish campaign, and some 500 served in the West in 1940.

The application of camouflage paint to vehicles was almost universally by using a standard spraygun. Most of the heavy armoured vehicles had engine-driven compressors that provided crews with adequate air pressure for painting. Almost all crews were responsible for painting their own equipment, and even when using standard shades a variety of colour density and coverage might be seen.

For the invasion of the Soviet Union in June 1941 virtually all equipment was painted dark grey. Ever hungry for motor transport for its still largely horse-drawn supply columns, the Wehrmacht pressed into service many hundreds of captured British and French vehicles. These too had been repainted in dark grey; but when captured Soviet trucks joined the transport parks many of them were simply left in their original Red Army green shade – although any salvaged tanks that were returned to use were repainted in German grey.

During the first four months of Operation 'Barbarossa' the grey vehicles, soon lightened by the sun and the ubiquitous dust of the steppes, blended in well with the terrain. However, with the onset of winter and the first snows at the end of October the Panzer crews became uncomfortably aware that they stood out sharply against the white background. Snow camouflage paint was one of the many items necessary for winter warfare which the overconfident Hitler had prevented the Wehrmacht from supplying. In mid November 1941 the Wehrmacht circulated an order for the use of water-soluble white paint and began to issue it, but unfortunately for the tank crews its distribution in the front lines was delayed for weeks. Consequently the Panzer units were forced to improvise in order to camouflage their vehicles, foraging locally for sources of rough limewash, or even chalk to rub on the grey steel; some photographs show attempts to break up the outlines of vehicles by tying on strips of white material, but many received no camouflage at all. The Red Army were old hands at winter concealment, of course, and during their massive counter-offensive of winter 1941/42 they profited from this.

With the spring thaw the white paint was washed off; but photographs from spring and summer 1942 show that a number of vehicles were being camouflaged with secondary colours daubed over the dark grey. The simplest methods were to paint on local mud and let it dry in streaks, and to attach bundles of long grass, hay or foliage, but there was also some use of available paints in greens and browns. It was in summer 1942 that the Panzers penetrated deep into semi-tropical southern Russia to reach the Caucasus; here the paints issued in North Africa would have been useful, and indeed some photographs clearly show the use in the southern USSR of yellow-brown (RAL 8000), red-brown (RAL 8017) or grey-green (RAL 7008)).

Opposite, above: Tanks from the advance party of 5.leichte Div (later redesignated 21.Pz Div) unloaded on the dockside in Tripoli, Libya, in March 1941. In the foreground, a PzKw II and a PzKw I still in dark grey finish both display on the right rear the yellow inverted-Y-and-two-bars sign of 3.Pz Div, which had provided 5.leichte Div with its Pz Regt 5 late in 1940. The tanks all display large red tactical numbers outlined in white; the partly visible 'R2'(?) identifies the PzKw I to the regimental headquarters echelon.

Opposite, below: Two PzKw IIIs of 5.leichte Div halted in the desert. Both are camouflaged in yellow-brown RAL 8000 with grey-green RAL 7008 blotches.

Above: An SdKfz 231 (8-rad) heavy armoured car on the North African coastline between Syrte and Mugtaa, March 1941. It has been painted in a scheme of grey-green RAL 7008 with a application of wavy lines in yellow-brown RAL 8000.

North Africa, 1941–43

The first vehicles to be sent to North Africa in February 1941, to put a halt to a succession of crushing British victories over the Italians, were shipped hastily in their original dark grey finish. Many were quickly camouflaged with mud, while awaiting the delivery of paint in suitable colours. An order of mid March 1941 specified these to be random, soft-edged applications of one-third grey-green (RAL 7008) over a base of two-thirds yellow-brown (RAL 7008); but the long and dangerous supply lines always made paint a low priority item, and many improvisations can be seen. Another factor was the extremely harsh environment, which soon bleached, peeled and sanded off the paint.

In late March 1942 new colours were specified: a base coat of a darker '*Afrika braun*' brown (RAL 8020) camouflaged with grey (RAL 7027). The former yellow-brown and grey-green remained in use until stocks ran out, and shortages continued to ensure that DAK vehicles presented an extremely battered and motley appearance. The capture of huge British stores of all kinds at Tobruk that June brought a welcome windfall of British Army 'light stone', 'pale cream' and 'deep cream'.

In the more temperate terrain of Tunisia in spring 1943 this motley range of colours was increased by the addition of olive-green (RAL 6003) – originally a colour issued for painting Luftwaffe buildings and ground equipment.

Three-colour camouflage, 1943–45

On 18 February 1943 an order specified that new vehicles and those in service were to be finished overall in dark yellow (RAL 7028). Although supplies to the front lines were always uncertain and variable, two secondary colours, olive-green (RAL 6003) and red-brown (RAL 8017), soon began to be issued. Provided in the form of concentrated pastes soluble with both water and petrol, these were to be diluted and applied at unit level, using sprayguns, brushes or mops. The range of appearance that it was possible to achieve to match local conditions thus became literally infinite, with colours depending upon local terrain, depth of shade upon degree of dilution, and patterns upon unit orders or even the whims of individual crews.

The useful flexibility built into this scheme failed, of course, to take account of the problems caused by either one of the possible solvents. If the pastes were let down with water, then heavy rain could wash them off; and in the last two years of the war fuel, which gave a more durable finish, increasingly became far too precious to waste on diluting paint. Units were forced to improvise, mixing the pastes with waste oil or other paints, which increased the huge range of variations in appearance, including such shades as brick-red, chocolate-brown and light green.

The deteriorating supply situation throughout 1944 led to many Panzers being seen finished in plain dark yellow. For the Ardennes offensive in December 1944 most German vehicles did not receive an application of white camouflage paste, and instead advanced through the snowy wooded hills of Belgium in overall dark yellow and various three-colour camouflage schemes. Given the air supremacy enjoyed by the Allies in 1944–45, the use of the most basic camouflage material of all – foliage – increased markedly, and was indeed believed to be the most important key to survival.

By contrast, with typical German ingenuity, new studies in the effectiveness of camouflage painting were even now seeing some AFVs reaching the front lines finished in newly modified patterns. These 'ambush' schemes were applied in particular to some Panther and Tiger II tanks and to Jagdpanzers such as Jagdpanzer IV, Jagdpanther and Hetzer. They used the usual three colours, often in large random areas, but each area was now covered with small spots of a contrasting colour, giving an effect like sun-dappled leaves.

Above: A PzKw III Ausf G or early H, at a maintenance workshop somewhere in Germany, summer 1941; the G model introduced the more powerful 5cm L/42 gun. The basic design dated from 1936, but it was repeatedly modified, and nearly a thousand were still in front line service at the opening of the Russian campaign in 1941. No markings are visible here on the overall dark grey RAL 7021 paint scheme, probably newly re-applied after repairs.

Opposite, top: A PzKw IV Ausf D on the long road into Russia, summer 1941. A rolled, camouflaged tarpaulin is stowed on the engine deck; this was primarily used for rigging a crew shelter while parked for the night in 'untactical' circumstances. The tank seems to be painted overall dark grey with blotches of brown, but this is hard to make out under the very heavy coating of road dust.

Opposite, below: Three grey-painted PzKw III Ausf Ls, clearly posed for maximum propaganda impact. Under magnification, each tank can be seen to display on the right side of the nose plate (as viewed) the yellow 'wolf-hook' sign of the SS-Div (mot) 'Das Reich'. The picture dates from summer 1942, almost certainly in France, where the badly mauled division was withdrawn that August for rebuilding as a Panzergrenadier formation. This was the period when the first three Waffen-SS divisions received the PzKw III Ausf L as their first significant allocations of armour.

Primary German AFV Colours, 1939–45

Black (RAL 9005)	Green (RAL 6007)
White 1 (RAL 9001)	Yellow (RAL 1006)
White 2 (RAL 9002)	Dark yellow (RAL 7028)
Ivory (RAL 1001)	Yellow-brown (RAL 8000)
Blue-grey (RAL 7016)	Africa-brown (RAL 8020)
Dark grey (RAL 7021)	Signal-brown (RAL 8002)
Grey (RAL 7027)	Red-brown (RAL 8017)
Field-grey (RAL 6006)	Red primer (RAL 8012)
Grey-green (RAL 7008)	Red (RAL 3000)
Olive-green (RAL 6003)	

Left: The shortage of white camouflage paint during the Wehrmacht's first winter in Russia led to improvisations, such as the dense scribbles of chalk rubbed all over the grey paintwork of this PzKw IV Ausf F1. (British private collection)

Below: By winter 1942/43 sufficient supplies of water-soluble whitewash reached the front. This 8-ton SdKfz 7 artillery tractor, crossing ground flooded by rain or melt water during that second winter, has received a thorough overall coating. By this time heavy, padded winter clothing could also be supplied, and the men riding in this half-track are warmly clad; note too their white-painted helmets.

Left: By the second winter of the Russian campaign the first sub-unit of PzKw VI Tigers – 1./sPz Abt 502 – had already been in action on the Leningrad front since the end of August, though at first with only four of them. At the end of September another five Tigers and 14 PzKw III Ausf Ns arrived with the company, and fought throughout the winter; they did not receive any replacements until February 1943. This Tiger of that unit has been completely coated with whitewash, covering all its markings.

Below: Another Tiger I Ausf E shows a less complete coat of snow camouflage, but this heavy streaking of white over the dark grey base coat does have the effect of confusing enemy gunners by breaking up its outline and thus confusing the 'perspective' when seen from a distance – as important as actual concealment, which can never be maintained if a tank has to move.

Right: An interesting photograph showing a StuG III Ausf G supporting Waffen-SS infantry during the Kursk offensive in July 1943, when all three of the premier SS divisions were committed. The StuG has a summer camouflage scheme of dark yellow RAL 7028 base colour, oversprayed with bands of olive green RAL 6003; note on the skirt armour plates the darker shade, presumably red-brown RAL 8017, applied on top of the green in dramatic zig-zags, perhaps by hand.

Below: In early winter 1944/5, the crew of a StuG III Ausf G from 2.SS-Pz Div 'Totenkopf' – identified by the left hand soldier's collar patch – tighten a tarpaulin over their vehicle for an overnight stay. It has been purposely parked next to a building in order to help conceal it, and the tarp will be pulled forward to hide at least part of the gun barrel – a tell-tale feature when seen from the air. Large areas of the three-colour summer camouflage scheme can be seen through the incomplete and fading coat of winter whitewash.

Right: Pioneer Sd Kfz 251/7 Ausf D bridge-laying half-tracks mounted on railway flat wagons for shipment to the front line in 1943. All of them appear to display the same summer camouflage scheme of dark yellow RAL 7028, oversprayed with a web of criss-crossing streaks of diluted olive green RAL 6003. No other markings are visible.

Below: During summer operations in 1944, the crews of two SdKfz 251/3 Ausf C command half-tracks (note the frame antennae) question two Soviet prisoners. Both vehicles are armed with the standard MG34 machine gun complete with an armoured shield. The half-track on the left has a camouflage pattern of yellow-brown RAL 8000 with widely spaced grey-green RAL 7008 blotches. The other has a base coat of dark yellow RAL 7028, oversprayed with a web pattern of fine lines in olive green RAL 6003.

Two rather more dramatic camouflage schemes applied at unit level.

Left: In a rail yard during a long-distance move in 1943, artillerymen pose on their Wespe self-propelled 10.5cm leFH 18/2 L/28 howitzer of a Panzerartillerie battalion. The only visible marking is the black-and-white national cross. The base coat of dark yellow RAL 7028 has been camouflaged with oversprayed spots and sweeping wavy bands of olive-green RAL 6003 and darker red-brown RAL 8017.

Below: This 3-ton SdKfz 11/4, crossing a Russian river towing a 7.5cm PaK 97/38 anti-tank gun, is boldly camouflaged with wide bands of olive-green over the base coat of dark yellow. The hard edges suggest that this overpainting was applied by hand with brushes rather than sprayed.

Above: Late 1943, and a Tiger I halts in a Russian village. The tactical number '323' is painted in red; it identifies a tank of 2.Zug, 3.Kompanie of sPz Abt 502. The camouflage of olive-green and red-brown over dark yellow is partly obscured by mud thrown up from the dirt roads (which almost hides the Balkenkreuz); the crew have purposely left the tank uncleaned, to enhance the camouflage effect. Note the difference between the well spaced loops of camouflage paint on the hull, and the very dense painting on the 8.8cm gun.

Right: A Tiger rolls along a Russian highway during winter 1943/44; hard frost made the going much easier than rain or thaw. Even following the costly German defeat at Kursk in July 1943, the Tigers continued to demonstrate their awesome killing power during the fierce defensive battles that followed. Battalions sometimes destroyed scores of Soviet tanks while fighting against huge odds.

Above: The camouflage on this SdKfz 251/9 Ausf C fire support half-track, photographed in 1943, has been crudely adapted. The vehicle appears to have a base coat of yellow-brown RAL 8000, with streaked traces of old whitewash on the engine compartment, concave side plates and gun shield. At a later date the crew have used a paintbrush to dot white paint over other areas of the side surfaces. Here, during a pause in operations, one of the crew is cleaning the bore of the short-barrelled 7.5cm KwK 37 L/24 howitzer.

Left: Summer 1944: note the foliage which is now much more necessary for this StuG III Ausf G than the swastika flag – any aircraft which suddenly appeared above the treetops was more likely to be an Ilyushin Stormovik or a P-47 Thunderbolt than a Messerschmitt. Although this is clearly only a temporary halt, a tarpaulin can also be seen on the roof and mantlet. This assault gun still has an intact set of *Schürzen*, and its thoroughly oversprayed three-colour summer scheme blends well with the terrain.

Left: A Waffen-SS assault gun moves up at Kursk, July 1943. Here the *Schürzen* show large, widely spaced, angular patches of RAL 6003 green and darker RAL 8017 brown applied in a 'splinter' pattern.

Below: Army Panzergrenadiers hitching a lift in early 1944, evidently far from the front – the gun still has its muzzle cover in place, there is no overhead camouflage, and nobody is watching the sky. This very heavy 'abstract painting' pattern of green and brown over the dark yellow features big blotches, dense groups of small dots, and curving streaks. Below the soldier grinning at the camera, note the Balkenkreuz apparently crudely repainted in solid black.

Above & right: The Panzerjäger Tiger (P) Elefant heavy tank destroyers, mounting the powerful 8.8cm PaK 43/2 L/71 gun, proved a disappointment when they went into action at Kursk in July 1943. Despite their lethal firepower – one gun knocked out Soviet tanks at more than three miles' range – their weight of 65 tons made them very slow, and the complexity of their dual engines and electronically controlled gearbox and steering made them prone to mechanical breakdowns, with many abandoned on the battlefield. All known photographs of the guns of sPz Jäg Regt 656 at Kursk show this dark yellow base coat with a web of olive-green or red-brown lines. The lower photograph shows the position of the black-and-white Balkenkreuz, and above it a faint white tactical number; this appears to be of two digits, although three-digit numbers are known to have been used by this regiment.

Above: The crew of another Elefant ensure that it is secure on a railway flat wagon for its long journey across Russia; it has received a light and patchy coat of winter whitewash over its summer camouflage. Those that survived Kursk were withdrawn, fitted with a hull machine gun, and later redeployed to Italy, where their crews had great difficulty in manoeuvring on narrow roads and weak bridges. A company of sPz Jäg Abt 590 were sent into action in February 1944 at Anzio, but again failed to achieve any great success.

Left: The unusual camouflage scheme applied to this StuG III Ausf G shows to advantage among sun-dappled birch trees. Comparison of shades suggests that a base coat of a darkish colour – red-brown – has been oversprayed with small groups of wavy lines of dark yellow and olive-green.

Above: Summer 1943: two Panzerjäger crewmen with their Marder III, based on the PzKw 38(t) chassis and armed with a 7.5cm PaK 40/3 anti-tank gun. Under the sparse foliage camouflage the only marking visible on the RAL 7028 finish is the Balkenkreuz; battery and troop designators are very rare in wartime photographs of these vehicles.

Left: The driver of another Marder III, this time in winter 1943. The vehicle seems to retain plain dark yellow finish, now with its outline slightly broken up with fir branches.

Opposite, above: The crew of this Luftwaffe SdKfz 7 tractor towing an 8.8cm Flak gun on the Western Front have cut an impressive mass of leafy branches.

Opposite, below: This Jagdpanzer 38(t) Hetzer tank-destroyer has been covered with equal care, by harvesting some kind of standing crop. Foliage matching the particular surroundings was obviously important for effective camouflage, but it had to be renewed frequently as it withered and changed colour.

Left: The *Zimmerit* pattern shows clearly in this shot of a Hungarian tank driver under instruction near Kolomea in spring 1944; the Tiger is red '114' of 1./sPz Abt 503. (British private collection)

Above: The US and British Tactical Air Forces completely ruled the skies at low altitude over the Western Front by autumn 1944, when this rather sparsely camouflaged Tiger I – probably of sPz Abt 506 – was photographed near Aachen, the first German city to fall to the Allied armies. This unit is taking an appreciable risk by making a road march in daylight.

ZIMMERIT

In August 1943, as the new three-colour camouflage was being introduced, the Army High Command (OKH) became worried by the possibility that the Red Army might acquire hand-placed magnetic anti-tank charges similar to their own 3kg Haft-Hohlladung shaped charge. To counter this, in December 1943 they ordered the application of a special anti-magnetic plaster coating (called *Zimmerit*, after its inventors Chemische Werke Zimmer GmbH) to many new AFVs leaving the factories, and to serving vehicles in the field. This provided a rough, textured coating that was patterned in various ways, thus denying the magnetic base of a charge a smooth contact with the steel.

Zimmerit was mixed from 40 per cent barium sulphate, which was not water-soluble; 25 per cent polyvinyl acetate – simple carpenters' white glue; 15 per cent ochre pigment; 10 per cent zinc sulphate and 10 per cent wood sawdust. The wet plaster was applied by hand to the vertical and sloped armour plates in an even layer about 5mm thick, which was left to dry for about four hours. A second, thinner coat was then applied with some kind of spatula, in a variety of ridged patterns, and finally dried with a blowtorch.

The order of December 1943 specified that *Zimmerit* was to be applied to all surfaces of the hull and superstructure, including surfaces under the armoured Schürzen. It was not to be applied to these skirt plates, the turret, external engine parts, tools, tracks, lamps or any similar areas. In fact *Zimmerit* was often applied to tank turrets, and sometimes to the Schürzen. It is seen in photographs on most tanks, assault guns and self-propelled tank destroyers, but rarely on armoured artillery or personnel carriers. (though at least one SdKfz 251 AusfD was photographed with a coat of plaster).

On 9 September 1944 *Zimmerit* application was ordered to be discontinued. There were (unfounded) concerns that it was inflammable under the impact of projectiles; more important was the fact that its utility was too doubtful to justify the cost and time. The Soviets never did produce a magnetic charge, although they used captured German munitions in some numbers.

The total weight of *Zimmerit* calculated as needed to cover the regulation surfaces of the various types of AFV to which it was applied was as follows; 1kg = 2.2lb:

PzKw III, StuG III, StuG IV, PzJäg 38(t) – 70kg

PzKw IV, PzJäg Marder – 100kg
FlakPz Wirbelwind, FlakPz Ostwind – 150kg
PzKw Panther, Bergepanther, Hummel, PzJäg Nashorn – 160kg
PzKw VI Tiger, Jagdpanther, Jagdpanzer IV/70 – 200kg
Sturmtiger, Jagdtiger – 250kg

The schematic artwork below illustrates typical patterns of *Zimmerit* application to the following types of AFVs, though some of these were very rarely seen:

(A) PzKw III, PzKw IV Ausf H & J, PzBefWg IV, PzKw V Panther, PzKw VI Tiger, StuG III, StuG IV, Brummbär, PzJäg IV/70, Wirbelwind, Ostwind, Panzersturmmörser, Jagdtiger

(B) PzKw IV Ausf H, PzKw V Panther Ausf G, StuG III Ausf G

(C) PzKw V Panther Ausf G

(D) StuG III, PzKw V Panther Ausf A & G

(E) StuG III, PzKw V Panther Ausf A & G, Jagdpanther

(F) StuG III Ausf G, StuH 42, PzKw V Panther, PzKw VI Tiger

(G) PzKw IV

(H) PzKw V Panther

(I) StuG III, PzKw V Panther Ausf G

(J) StuG III

(K) PzKw V Panther, isolated example SdKfz 251 Ausf D

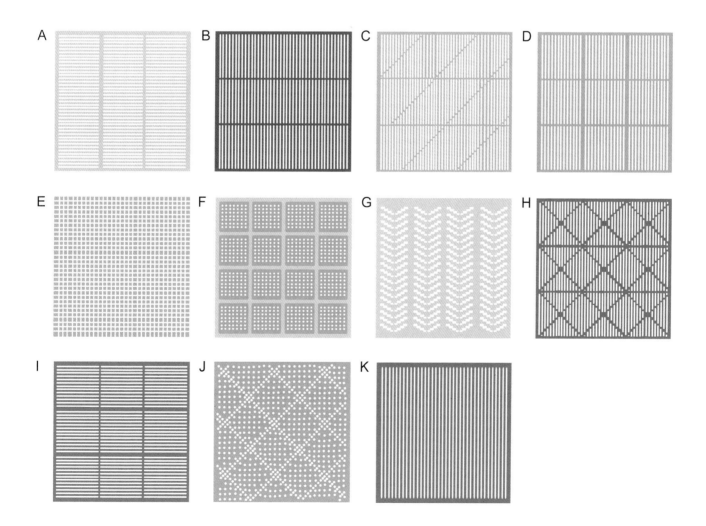

Left: A column of Waffen-SS StuG IVs parked by a French roadside in spring 1944, before the Normandy landings; several SS divisions were resting and working up in France during that period. The vehicles have received a coat of *Zimmerit* plaster and are simply finished in dark yellow paint; the only marking is the national cross on the side of the driver's compartment. While this unit is unidentified, similar-looking StuG IVs of SS-Pz Abt 17 'Götz von Berlichingen' were knocked out by US 2nd Arm Div tanks south-west of Carentan on 13 June.

Below: US troops examine a knocked-out PzKw V Panther Ausf G beside a Normandy hedgerow. This photograph clearly shows the characteristic *Zimmerit* pattern of horizontal rows of vertical ridges and grooves often seen on the Panther. Patches of darker camouflage paint can be seen over the dark yellow base coat; less visible is the ghostly tactical number '215' painted in large red digits, outlined white, on the turret side.

Left: An interesting photo showing a crew member of a Tiger II ('King Tiger') spraying streaks of red-brown or olive-green secondary camouflage over the glacis. Note the factory-applied coat of *Zimmerit* under the base coat of dark yellow RAL 7028 paint. The plaster has even been worked into neat ridges on the compound curves around the hull machine gun position.

Below: A knocked-out Jagdpanzer IV/70 tank destroyer in summer 1944. This view emphasizes the very low height – only 6ft 1in – which enabled it to take advantage of every slight fold in the ground. Over the coat of *Zimmerit* it has been finished in the so-called 'ambush' scheme which imitated sun dappling through the leaves of woodland – where German AFVs now had to spend so much time in concealment. The overspray of olive-green and red-brown almost covers the dark yellow, particularly in the frontal areas, and small dots of dark yellow can be seen over the secondary colours on the hull sides. The faint three-digit tactical number seems to be '300', stencilled in black or dark red.

8. LICENCE PLATES

WITH the exception of tanks and other fully-tracked AFVs, all German military vehicles including wheeled and half-tracked armour were assigned a number that was displayed on licence plates, exactly as were the civilian vehicles with which they shared the roads of Germany, and later the occupied countries. The Army, which before the Nazis came to power had used the prefix 'RW' for Reichswehr, switched to 'WH' for Wehrmacht Heer; the Navy used 'WM' for Wehrmacht Marine; the Air Force, 'WL' for Wehrmacht Luftwaffe. The Waffen-SS used a simple 'SS' prefix, because when the system was first devised the SS was not a part of the armed forces. Since the Polizei also used many types of military vehicles, note for elimination purposes that their licence plate prefix was 'POL'.

Before the outbreak of war the **Army** allocated blocks of licence plate numbers to the regional Wehrkreis or military districts into which the Reich was divided. These blocks, with the location of the Wehrkreis headquarters, were are follows:

Wehrkreis I (Königsberg)	WH 10000–19999
Wehrkreis II (Stettin)	WH 20000–29999
Wehrkreis III (Berlin)	WH 30000–39999
Wehrkreis IV (Dresden)	WH 40000–49999
Wehrkreis V (Stuttgart)	WH 50000–59999
Wehrkreis VI (Münster)	WH 60000–69999
Wehrkreis VII (Munich)	WH 70000–79999
Wehrkreis VIII (Breslau)	WH 80000–89999
Wehrkreis IX (Kassel)	WH 90000–99999
Wehrkreis X (Hamburg)	WH 100000–109999
Wehrkreis XI (Hanover)	WH 110000–119999
Wehrkreis XII (Wiesbaden)	WH 120000–129999
Wehrkreis XIII (Nürnberg)	WH 130000–139999
Wehrkreis XIV (Magdeburg)	WH 140000–149999, and WH 240000–249999
Wehrkreis XV (Jena)	WH 150000–159999, and WH 250000–259999
Wehrkreis XVI (Berlin)	WH 160000–169999, and WH 260000–269999
Wehrkreis XVII (Linz/Donau)	WH 170000–179999
Wehrkreis XVIII (Salzburg)	WH 180000–189999

The Panzer and Light divisions were all stationed in Wehrkreis XIV, XV and XVI, as assets of the pre-war Armeekorps which bore the same numbers.

The **Navy** regional commands were also allocated blocks of numbers, as follows: Oberkommando der Kriegsmarine (Berlin), WM 1–999; Kdo der Marinestation Ostsee (Kiel), WM 1000–29999; Kdo der Marinestation Nordsee (Wilhelmshaven) WM 30000–59999.

Those allocated to **Air Force** regional commands were:

Luftgaukommando I (Königsburg)	WL 10000–19999
Luftgaukdo–See (Kiel)	WL 20000–29999
Luftgaukdo III (Berlin)	WL 300000–319999
Luftgaukdo IV (Dresden)	WL 400000–409999
Luftgaukdo VI (Münster)	WL 600000–609999
Luftgaukdo VII (Munich)	WL 700000–709999

Above: At some date after February 1934, a light field car follows an SdKfz 7 half-track towing part of a 17cm sK 18cm or 21cm Mörser 18. The licence plate of the Horch is marked 'RW 15052', for 'Reichswehr'. Although this title for the armed forces changed to 'Wehrmacht' in 1935, it was not until 1939 that the last licence plates were altered.

Luftgaukdo VIII (Breslau)	WL 800000–809999
Luftgaukdo XI (Hanover)	WL 110000–119999
Luftgaukdo XIII (Nürnberg)	WL 130000–139999
Luftgaukdo XVII (Vienna)	WL 170000–179999

After the outbreak of war, replacement vehicles at first continued to receive numbers in these blocks for the units whose home depots remained in the relevant Wehrkreis. With time, however, the system became more complicated, as hundreds of thousands of vehicles were added to the pre-war inventories; the numbers passed the million mark in 1944, and new blocks began to be allocated randomly.

A major contribution to this problem was the impressment of large numbers of captured foreign vehicles. Military vehicles taken into German military service were given Wehrmacht numbers; but many civilian cars were also swept up for use by the military, and to save trouble these retained their civilian licence plates, but received a prominently marked 'WH' in white, black or yellow, often on a front wing.

After the outbreak of war, licence plates with special prefixes were allocated for use by the German civil and military government authorities in the various **occupied territories**. Examples for military authorities are as follows (civil administrations used the prefix 'Z' in place of the 'M'):

Belgium & Northern France – MB
Denmark – MD
France – MF
Poland – MG
Holland – MW
Norway – MN
'Ostland', i.e. Baltic states – MO
Military mission to Romania – MR
'Südost', i.e. western Russia – MS
Ukraine – MU

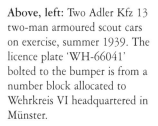

Above, left: Two Adler Kfz 13 two-man armoured scout cars on exercise, summer 1939. The licence plate 'WH-66041' bolted to the bumper is from a number block allocated to Wehrkreis VI headquartered in Münster.

Above, right: This pre-war Bussing-Nag truck taken into the Wehrmacht keeps its civilian licence number prefix 'IY', identifying the city of Düsseldorf. 'WH' has been crudely painted on the width indicator bar, and the maker's name on the bumper, for quick identification by military transport personnel.

Examples of the blocks used by Navy authorities were: Commanding Admiral, France (Paris) – WM 60000–79999; Commanding Admiral, Norway (Oslo) – WM 80000–99999.

During 1940–44 the plates used in the occupied territories remained unchanged; but by December 1944 all or much of these countries had been liberated by the Allies. In that month all the national prefixes were ordered discontinued except for those for Norway, Denmark, Poland (the so-called 'General Government') and Holland. (At the same date the previously independent construction service, Organization Todt, was taken within the Wehrmacht and exchanged its old 'OT' plates for 'WT'.)

*　　*　　*

Physically, the licence plates were made from stamped sheet metal, most being attached to the vehicles by bolts or by separate metal frames or struts. They were normally painted white with black letters and numbers, and a black outer rim.

The front plate was conventionally a single strip 475mm long by 90mm deep, with the prefix and numbers marked in a single line. The rear plate came in two minor variations. Early plates were 320mm wide by 200mm deep, with clipped top corners; the two- or three-letter prefix was painted in a short top row and the numbers below this. Later-war plates lacked the clipped corners. The rectangular rear-format plate was attached to the front of some types of vehicles, however.

Motorcycles had specially designed smaller plates, the front one being curved to match the profile of the mudguard and the rear one being less than half the size of the standard rear plate.

After 1941, many photographs show vehicles – particularly, but not exclusively armoured types – with the licence numbers painted instead directly on to a vehicle surface, in which cases the black rim was often omitted. Occasionally, instead of being painted in black on a white strip, numbers were seen painted in white on the vehicle's camouflage-painted surface.

While the licence numbers, visible at a distance, were adequate for most purposes, there was a further security measure. This allowed military and field police checkpoints to confirm the legitimate use of vehicles (especially in rear areas and occupied territories) by comparing an additional vehicle marking against the driver's travel documents. Every military unit down to Abteilung level – and in some cases, even to Kompanie – was identified in the military bureaucracy by a field post number, for use by the military postal service. It was standard practice to stamp this *Feldpostnummer* on each licence plate of every one of the unit's vehicles. The stamp is sometimes visible in close-up photographs as a circular mark between the prefix letters and the digits. It was stamped in indelible red (occasionally, black) ink, and bore the eagle-and-swastika national emblem below the word *Dienststelle* and above *Feldpostnummer* and the numerals.

Right: An SdKfz 10 half-track (apparently one of those built by Cottbus Mechanische Werke GmbH) demonstrates its obstacle-crossing abilities on a steep earth bank. The licence plate 'WH-31347' (Wehrkreis III, Berlin) is attached to a bar in front of the radiator. The overall finish is dark grey RAL 7021 with dark brown No.45 blotches.

Left: An early production SdKfz 251 – immaculately clean, unstowed, and clearly the pride and joy of the young Schütze posing in it. The licence number 'WH-193260' (from a block not immediately identifiable) is stencilled directly on to the front armour.

Right: The leading SdKfz 251 in this dusty column in Russia, summer 1942, has its engine cover plates open – an overheating problem? Again, it shows a painted-on licence number ('WH-19375' – Wehrkreis I, Königsburg). Visible, but illegible, in the shadow of the engine plate, is an unofficial name added by the crew in Gothic script – 'Benny'? Naming vehicles was not as common as in Allied armies, but far from unknown.

Above: This Horch (which may belong to Inf Lehr Regt (mot), attached to 10.Pz Div) has halted on a main road in France in May 1940. Wider vehicles typically carried two licence plates – here 'WH-276081' of an unidentified block. Note the normal early war clipped-corner format.

Left: Large vehicles also carried a pair of front number plates, at each end of the bumper – as demonstrated by this SdKfz 7 gun tractor of a Luftwaffe Flak unit in Russia, 1941. Mounted on each wing, the extended rod with a ball on the end (which was normally painted white) was the usual width reminder for Wehrmacht drivers. The licence number 'WL-408251' is from a block allocated to Luftgau IV, headquartered in Dresden.

Left: A BMW motorcycle combination crew, with a senior NCO riding pillion, show deep suntans and a plentiful scattering of road-dust. The curved front licence plate 'WH-28814' shows that their home depot is in Wehrkreis II (Stettin).

Below: A striking study of two officers of 1.SS-Pz Div 'Leibstandarte-SS Adolf Hitler' using a motorcycle combination (licence plate 'SS-302608') during anti-partisan sweeps in Italy in September 1943. The 'LAH' was the only one of the 'senior' SS divisions to serve in Italy; it was pulled back from the Russian Front in the aftermath of Kursk to help disarm the Italian army after the overthrow of Mussolini.

Above: An interesting photograph showing a Waffen-SS motorcyclist of the 'LAH' riding an Army motorcycle with the licence plate 'WH-614785' during Army Group Centre's summer campaign in 1941. Two SS officers confer over maps beside the field car.

Right: This SdKfz 7 half-track advancing with Guderian's Panzergruppe 2 in summer 1941 carries the numberplate 'SS-9517'. It belongs to the SS-Div (mot) 'Reich', whose yellow 'wolf-hook' sign can be made out under a thick layer of dust on the left wing, opposite the white 'G'. Above the divisional sign is the tactical symbol of a motorized infantry platoon and '1'. This identifies these troops to 1.Kompanie of either SS-Standarte 'Deutschland' or 'Der Führer'. It is interesting that an SS unit should have received the SdKfz 7 as a personnel carrier, a role for which this large prime mover was considerably over-powered.

9. PENNANTS, SIGNAL FLAGS & VICTORY MARKINGS

Above: Army officers atop their SdKfz 251/3 Ausf C half-track, fitted with a frame aerial for the command radio set. The triangular tin command pennant in the right foreground, painted in black over white over red, identifies one of the divisional staff vehicles.

GERMAN command pennants were mounted on the left wing of headquarters vehicles, or dismounted and displayed on ground poles, to show the location of unit and formation commanders and to identify – by a clear visual code – their level and branch of command. The pennants were normally of heavy cloth held rigid by rods, or (more usually in wartime) of thin metal, painted in several colours; the design might also simply be painted on the surface of a vehicle:

Army group command Square flag; centre, vertically/horizontally quartered black (top hoist, bottom fly) and white; red inner border; white outer border.

Army command The same, without white outer border.

Panzergruppe command Square flag; centre, diagonally quartered black (top & bottom) and white; red border.

Army corps command Horizontal rectangular flag; diagonally quartered white (both side triangles), black (top) and red (bottom); no border.

Divisional command Triangular pennant; three equal horizontal stripes of black, over white, over red. Divisional sign or other marking sometimes added to white stripe.

Command flags from brigade downwards featured branch-of-service colours (Waffenfarben); the relevant colours were:

Panzertruppe & Panzerjäger – rose-pink

Panzergrenadiere – grass-green

Infanterie (other than Pz Gren) – white

Artillerie – red

Aufklärungstruppe – bright yellow

Brigade command Triangular pennant; three equal horizontal stripes of black, Waffenfarbe, black.

Regimental command Horizontal rectangular flag; three equal horizontal stripes of black, Waffenfarbe, black.

Battalion command Triangular pennant; three equal horizontal stripes of Waffenfarbe, black, Waffenfarbe. Some units might be differenced by an equal-width black vertical stripe crossing the pennant in the centre. Tactical symbols, Roman numerals for Abteilungen, and even the commander's name might be added to parts of the pennant in contrasting black or white.

Example: The command pennant of Maj Helmut Ritgen, commanding II Abt/ Pz Lehr Regt 130 in Normandy, was striped pink, black, pink. On the top pink stripe was a black open rhombus enclosing the script 'L' of the division. On the black stripe was the name *Ritgen* in white italics. On the bottom pink stripe was the battalion's white square crossed by two diagonal red lines (high right, low left).

Rank pennants were also mounted on the vehicles of general officers, on the right wing, either alone or opposite any command pennant. These were of heavy cloth, usually held rigid by a rod frame or protected by a stiff, clear cellophane cover; they were to be covered if the commander was not personally present. Pre-23 April 1941 they were grey, 20cm on the hoist and 30cm on the fly, bearing in silver a spread-wing eagle-and-swastika national emblem and an embroidered border. After that date the emblem and border were gold and the latter more elaborate, patterned with tiny swastikas (the old type was retained for senior field officers and officials). From that date also a new 30cm-square pennant was introduced for the rank of field marshal, with a grey outer and gold inner border enclosing a gold folded-wing eagle-and-swastika above crossed batons.

* * *

Since few pre-war armoured vehicles were fitted with radios a system of passing basic messages with hand-held **signal flags** was devised, and these continued in use to some extent, particularly in the first half of the war. The usual size of the flag was a rectangle 30cm by 40cm. The meanings of the signals could differ depending upon their movement, and over time. Space prevents more than a few examples here:

Yellow flag In 1940, raised upright it meant 'Follow me'; in 1941, 'Conform on me'. In 1940, raised and lowered vertically it meant 'Extended order'; waved side to side, 'Single file'.

Blue flag In 1940, upright meant 'Double file'; in 1941, 'Extend'. In 1940, raised and lowered meant 'Close up'; waved side to side, 'Form arrowhead'; held slanting downwards, 'Open out'.

Red flag In 1940, held upright meant 'Stand by'; in 1941, 'Attack' or 'Attack individually'. In 1940, raised and lowered meant 'Ready for action'; waved side to side, 'Attack artillery and tanks'. Both these last examples suggest that momentary confusion might have dire consequences.

Halved yellow-over-red flag In 1940, held upright meant 'Take up position'; in 1941, 'Get hull down'; in 1940–41, waved side to side meant 'Form broad arrowhead, base leading'.

Halved yellow-over-blue In 1941, held upright meant 'Right wheel', and waved side to side, 'Left wheel'.

Halved blue-over-red In 1940, held upright meant 'Take cover'; in 1941, waved side to side meant 'About turn', or simply 'Move'.

Less potentially confusing, a *yellow flag with a thick black cross* either held upright or waved side to side meant either 'Am broken down/ a casualty' or just 'I need assistance'. However, in North Africa in early 1942, Pz Regt 5 used a red, white and red flag to indicate that a tank was damaged. A flag not much seen in photographs was the triangular sub-unit headquarters location pennant – yellow with a small red cross surrounded by a thick black border.

*   *   *

While never officially recognized – and indeed, sometimes vainly forbidden by higher authority – the display of 'kills' – **victory tally markings** – was widespread on armoured vehicles and artillery pieces.

Sometimes these were simple barrel rings; sometimes, particularly on artillery gun shields, more elaborate displays indicated what type of targets were claimed as destroyed. Barrel markings were normally painted in a contrasting colour, usually white on dark grey barrels, and black, red or white on desert brown and – from 1943 – on dark yellow. While not common, some tallies were seen painted in several different colours simul-taneously, probably to indicate different types of targets or kills in different theatres of operations; these were more often seen on the Eastern Front and in Italy. Some barrel tallies even imitated the tailfin scoreboards of Luftwaffe fighter pilots by including a tiny painted 'label' with the date, type or nationality of the target claimed.

Some tank and artillery crews saw extensive action over several years, and as a result ran up such sizeable scores that they had to modify the method of recording kills in order to fit them on the gun barrel. Again, they would follow the lead of Luftwaffe aces and 'consolidate' past kills; the pilots did so with symbols of their decorations and the total score which earned them; the tank men, by consolidating kills in groups of fives or tens indicated by wider rings, periodically painting out another batch of thin rings and adding a single thick one. By no means all the ace tank commanders followed this practice – if for no other reason than simply because they changed their actual vehicles so often, and it would have been ridiculous (or impossible) to repaint each new mount. Even so, some of them did accumulate scores of over 100 kills; and these might be painted on a tank for a 'photo opportunity' when the Propagandakompanien came to record the award of the Knight's Cross, or some similar excuse for celebration.

Photographs quite often show victory tallies on Flak gun shields, particularly those of larger weapons like the 8.8cm. These usually take the form of silhouettes – of tanks, aircraft, even boats – followed by accumulating rows of little bars.

Victory displays became – paradoxically – less common late in the war. The reason was partly that the hard-pressed Wehrmacht was increasingly conscious of the need for camouflage and concealment; and partly that very few of the highest scoring crews survived until the last few months. However, such displays were always recognized at unit level as good for morale – of the new recruits, as much as the veterans themselves – and were seldom very strictly discouraged.

Right: North Africa, summer 1941: a Panzerbefehlswagen III command tank of 15. or 21.Pz Div moving along the coastal highway. The tank is heavily loaded with stores, but what might appear to be a stowage rack on the engine deck is in fact the 'bedstead' aerial for the extra radio equipment – this vehicle could carry up to six sets. The gun and mantlet are dummies cast in a light alloy. A cloth divisional command pennant flies from the rod antenna. The only visible marking is the DAK sign inset from the hull machine gun; this type sometimes also displayed a white outline Balkenkreuz centred on this bolt-on front armour. The tank is camouflaged with indistinct areas of grey-green RAL 7008 over yellow-brown RAL 8000.

Right: The use of a dismounted command pennant in Russia. The fur-lined grey hooded parkas worn by these troops from SS-Pz Gren Div 'Totenkopf' suggest that this is the winter of 1942/43. In the left background, left of the Army liaison officer, a metal battalion command pennant is striped white, black, white – the Waffen-SS mechanized infantry always kept their white Infanterie Waffenfarbe in place of the green of Army Panzergrenadiere. The black 'II' on the top white stripe identifies this as a staff element of II Abteilung of either 1. or 3.SS-Totenkopf Infanterie Regimente.

Below: A draft horse helps to un-bog a field car from the Russian mud. There is a battalion command pennant in stripes of a pale Waffenfarbe and black painted on the rear. In two places we see the yellow anchor sign of the Hamburg-raised 20.Inf Div (mot), later 20.Pz Gren Div; so this is probably a vehicle from either Inf Regt 73 or 90. The large open circle symbol is unexplained.

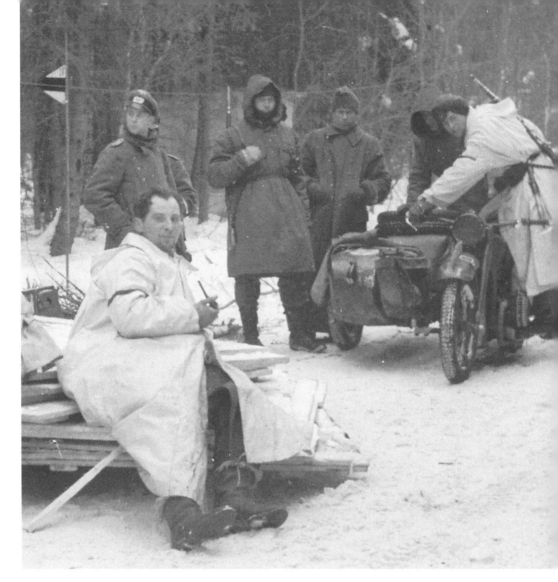

Above: A general officer is saluted by one of his Panzer officers as he alights from a staff car, which seems to fly the first type rank pennant in silver on grey. However, he carries a field marshal's undress baton. His features strongly resemble photos of GenObst von Kluge, the commander of 4.Armee during the 1940 French campaign. Kluge was promoted to field marshal in July 1941, which should have entitled him to the new April 1941 pattern of GFM's rank flag – but no military regulation is ever universally obeyed at once.

Right: The driver poses next to a civilian car that has been taken into Luftwaffe service as a staff car. Although many such vehicles retained their original licence plates, this one has been allocated a Luftwaffe plate – and note the circular field post office stamp between 'WL' and the numbers. Attached to the left wing is a Luftwaffe general officer's rank pennant in blue-grey cotton fabric with an internal wire frame. It is double-sided, with a gold-embroidered Luftwaffe eagle and border.

Left: The commander of a late-model StuG III pulls himself up smartly as he recognizes the command insignia on the snow-camouflaged staff car that has just pulled up beside his assault gun. On its left front bumper it displays the diagonally-quartered black, red and white pennant of an Armeekorps command, and from behind the right headlight it flies the personal rank pennant of the commanding general. (Note that this is an impressed civilian car, painted on the right wing with the Army's 'WH'.)

Opposite: A splendid close-up of a StuG III Ausf B crossing a river during early operations in Russia, summer 1941. The dusty grey assault gun already shows off eight victory rings round its stubby howitzer barrel. Incidentally, this photo gives an excellent view of the tapering 'trench' left of the gun mantlet, which led back to the gunner's frontal sight aperture; this obvious shot-trap was eliminated on the Ausf C and later marks.

Opposite: A blurred 1942 photo showing the Horch field car of Gen Erwin Rommel, who stands beside the rear wheel. The white DAK sign can be seen on the front door; note general officer's pennant on the right front wing; and the Panzerarmee Afrika command flag (quartered black, red and white) on the left. The car may be 'WH-1041788', which still survives in a private collection.

Right: A cine frame from an earlier date: note the diagonally-quartered flag with a wide red border denoting an Armeekorps command. Rommel's has been illustrated as quartered black at the top, white both sides, and red at the bottom with the word 'AFRIKA' in black, but there is no sign of this here. The rear of the car carries an Italian Army licence plate, 'RE-3/0863'. Note the DAK sign to the left of this, and an outline command pennant to the right.

Above: Excellent uniform details in a propaganda photo of a Knight's Cross holder, Oblt Ludwig, 'conferring with his battery officers' in Normandy, 1944; they wear a mixture of Panzerjäger and Sturmartillerie insignia. More to the immediate point, note the white 'kill' rings round the barrel of Ludwig's camouflaged StuG, carefully exposed for the photographer: one wide and 16 narrow.

Right: An SdKfz 7 anti-aircraft half-track mounting the quadruple 2cm Flak 38 cannon, probably in the winter of 1942/43. On the dark grey gun shield the white victory tally shows clearly: the silhouettes of some kind of vehicle with 15 bars beside it, and of an aircraft with 20.

Two examples of 8.8cm dual-purpose guns of Flak units being towed by SdKfz 7 half-tracks.

Left: There are 14 victory rings behind the muzzle, showing clearly in white. Far less evident are what seem to be a continuous series of rings of the same proportions but in a much less contrasting shade, which appear to fill the entire barrel back to the travelling brace – at least twice as many again.

Below: In this winter scene from 1943 we get a better view of the Flak 36/37 gun and the SdAh 203 limber. The half-track is painted in dark yellow RAL 7028, but the gun and limber are still in dark grey, neither with any apparent whitewash camouflage. The gun shield shows an impressive kill tally, arranged under different silhouettes: an aircraft with 12 bars; an AFV with 15; something obscure (perhaps softskin transport?) with 7; and finally, a solitary credit for destroying an observation balloon – the Red Army still used manned balloons.

Right: Two men hooded – and in one case masked – against the cruel Russian winter are photographed behind the MG 42 machine gun of their SdKfz 251 half-track. The shield displays a very large and carefully painted tally of victories, which must have been good for unit pride. The numbered columns are unexplained, but the kills are clearly 8 landing craft, 2 tanks, 2 trucks, an observation balloon and a seaplane.

Below: A meticulous 8.8cm-gun crewman brings the victory record up to date with a specially cut stencil. He adds a steamer to the 4 bunkers, 4 artillery pieces, and 19 unspecified kills which his crew already boast.